enVision® Mathematics

Volume 1 Topics 1-7

Authors

Randall I. Charles
Professor Emeritus
Department of Mathematics
San Jose State University
San Jose, California

Jennifer Bay-Williams
Professor of Mathematics Education
College of Education and Human
Development
University of Louisville
Louisville, Kentucky

Robert Q. Berry, III
Professor of Mathematics Education
Department of Curriculum,
Instruction and Special Education
University of Virginia
Charlottesville, Virginia

Janet H. Caldwell
Professor Emerita
Department of Mathematics
Rowan University
Glassboro, New Jersey

Zachary Champagne
Assistant in Research
Florida Center for Research in Science,
Technology, Engineering, and
Mathematics (FCR-STEM)
Jacksonville, Florida

Juanita Copley
Professor Emerita, College of Education
University of Houston
Houston, Texas

Warren Crown
Professor Emeritus of Mathematics
Education
Graduate School of Education
Rutgers University
New Brunswick, New Jersey

Francis (Skip) Fennell
Professor Emeritus of
Education and Graduate and
Professional Studies
McDaniel College
Westminster, Maryland

Karen Karp
Professor of
Mathematics Education
School of Education
Johns Hopkins University
Baltimore, Maryland

Stuart J. Murphy
Visual Learning Specialist
Boston, Massachusetts

Jane F. Schielack
Professor Emerita
Department of Mathematics
Texas A&M University
College Station, Texas

Jennifer M. Suh
Associate Professor for
Mathematics Education
George Mason University
Fairfax, Virginia

Jonathan A. Wray
Mathematics Supervisor
Howard County Public Schools
Ellicott City, Maryland

SAVVAS
LEARNING COMPANY

ISBN-13: 978-0-13-495363-2
ISBN-10: 0-13-495363-0
13 2023

Digital Resources

Go to SavvasRealize.com

You'll be using these digital resources throughout the year!

 Interactive Student Edition
Access online or offline.

 Interactive Additional Practice Workbook
Access online or offline.

 Math Tools
Explore math with digital tools.

Assessment
Show what you've learned.

 Visual Learning
Interact with visual learning animations.

 Videos
Watch Math Practices Animations, Another Look Videos, and clips to support 3-Act Math.

 Games
Play math games to help you learn.

 Activity
Solve a problem and share your thinking.

 Practice Buddy
Do interactive practice online.

 Glossary
Read and listen in English and Spanish.

SAVVAS
realize™ Everything you need for math anytime, anywhere

Contents

Digital Resources at SavvasRealize.com

TOPICS

1. Understand Addition and Subtraction

2. Fluently Add and Subtract Within 10

3. Addition Facts to 20: Use Strategies

4. Subtraction Facts to 20: Use Strategies

5. Work with Addition and Subtraction Equations

6. Represent and Interpret Data

7. Extend the Counting Sequence

8. Understand Place Value

9. Compare Two-Digit Numbers

10. Use Models and Strategies to Add Tens and Ones

11. Use Models and Strategies to Subtract Tens

12. Measure Lengths

13. Time and Money

14. Reason with Shapes and Their Attributes

15. Equal Shares of Circles and Rectangles

And remember your Interactive Student Edition is available at SavvasRealize.com!

SavvasRealize.com

This shows how you can add the parts to find the sum.

$4 + 2 = \square$

TOPIC 1
Understand Addition and Subtraction

enVision® STEM Project 1
Review What You Know. 2
Pick a Project 3
3-ACT MATH Preview: Grab a Bite 4

1-1 Add To 5

1-2 Put Together 9

1-3 Both Addends Unknown 13

1-4 Take From 17

1-5 Compare Situations. 21

1-6 More Compare Situations 25

1-7 Change Unknown 29

1-8 Practice Adding and Subtracting 33

1-9 PROBLEM SOLVING Construct Arguments 37

Fluency Review Activity 41
Vocabulary Review. 42
Reteaching 43
Topic Assessment Practice 47
Topic Performance Task 51

You can think addition to subtract.

$$7 - 3 = \boxed{?}$$

$$3 + \boxed{?} = 7$$

TOPIC 2
Fluently Add and Subtract Within 10

enVision® STEM Project 53
Review What You Know 54
Pick a Project 55

2-1   **Count On to Add** 57

2-2   **Doubles** 61

2-3   **Near Doubles** 65

2-4   **Facts with 5 on a Ten-Frame** 69

2-5   **Add in Any Order** 73

2-6   **Count Back to Subtract** 77

2-7   **Think Addition to Subtract** 81

2-8   **Solve Word Problems with Facts to 10** 85

2-9   **PROBLEM SOLVING Look For and Use Structure** 89

Fluency Practice Activity 93
Vocabulary Review 94
Reteaching 95
Topic Assessment Practice 99
Topic Performance Task 103

SavvasRealize.com

You can use different ways to remember addition facts.

Doubles   Near Doubles

Make 10

TOPIC 3
Addition Facts to 20: Use Strategies

enVision® STEM Project 105
Review What You Know. 106
Pick a Project 107
3-ACT MATH Preview: Go for a Spin. 108

3-1   Count On to Add 109

3-2   Count On to Add Using an Open Number Line. 113

3-3   Doubles. 117

3-4   Doubles Plus. 121

3-5   Make 10 to Add 125

3-6   Continue to Make 10 to Add. 129

3-7   Explain Addition Strategies. 133

3-8   Solve Addition Word Problems with Facts to 20. 137

3-9   PROBLEM SOLVING Critique Reasoning. 141

Fluency Practice Activity. 145
Vocabulary Review. 146
Reteaching. 147
Topic Assessment Practice 151
Topic Performance Task 155

You can count back to solve subtraction problems.

$10 - 3 =$ ___7___

TOPIC 4
Subtraction Facts to 20: Use Strategies

enVision® STEM Project. 157
Review What You Know. 158
Pick a Project 159

4-1   **Count to Subtract** 161

4-2   **Make 10 to Subtract**. 165

4-3   **Continue to Make 10 to Subtract** 169

4-4   **Fact Families**. 173

4-5   **Use Addition to Subtract** 177

4-6   **Continue to Use Addition to Subtract** 181

4-7   **Explain Subtraction Strategies** 185

4-8   **Solve Word Problems with Facts to 20**. 189

4-9   **PROBLEM SOLVING Reasoning** 193

Fluency Practice Activity. 197
Vocabulary Review. 198
Reteaching 199
Topic Assessment Practice 203
Topic Performance Task 207

SavvasRealize.com

You can add three numbers in different ways.

TOPIC 5
Work with Addition and Subtraction Equations

enVision® STEM Project 209
Review What You Know 210
Pick a Project 211
3-ACT MATH Preview: Weighed Down 212

5-1 Find the Unknown Numbers 213

5-2 True or False Equations 217

5-3 Make True Equations 221

5-4 Add Three Numbers 225

5-5 Word Problems with Three Addends 229

5-6 Solve Addition and Subtraction Word Problems 233

5-7 PROBLEM SOLVING Precision 237

Fluency Practice Activity 241
Vocabulary Review 242
Reteaching 243
Topic Assessment Practice 245
Topic Performance Task 247

Contents

You can show data in a tally chart.

Black	Red	Blue
卌	||||	||

TOPIC 6
Represent and Interpret Data

enVision® STEM Project 249
Review What You Know 250
Pick a Project 251

6-1   Organize Data Into Three Categories 253

6-2   Collect and Represent Data 257

6-3   Interpret Data 261

6-4   Continue to Interpret Data 265

6-5   PROBLEM SOLVING Make Sense and Persevere 269

Fluency Practice Activity 273
Vocabulary Review 274
Reteaching 275
Topic Assessment Practice 277
Topic Performance Task 279

SavvasRealize.com

Counting above 100 is just like counting below 100.

100, 101

TOPIC 7
Extend the Counting Sequence

enVision® STEM Project 281
Review What You Know. 282
Pick a Project 283
3-ACT MATH Preview: Super Selfie. 284

7-1 Count by 10s to 120. 285

7-2 Count by 1s to 120. 289

7-3 Count on a Number Chart to 120 293

7-4 Count by 1s or 10s to 120 297

7-5 Count on an Open Number Line. 301

7-6 Count and Write Numerals 305

7-7 PROBLEM SOLVING Repeated Reasoning 309

Fluency Practice Activity. 313
Vocabulary Review. 314
Reteaching 315
Topic Assessment Practice 317
Topic Performance Task 319

Contents

TOPIC 8 in volume 2
Understand Place Value

enVision® STEM Project.................................... 321

Review What You Know.................................... 322

Pick a Project 323

8-1 Make Numbers 11 to 19 325

8-2 Numbers Made with Tens 329

8-3 Count with Groups of Tens and Ones 333

8-4 Tens and Ones 337

8-5 Continue with Tens and Ones 341

8-6 Different Names for the Same Number.................. 345

8-7 PROBLEM SOLVING Look For and Use Structure 349

Fluency Practice Activity................................. 353

Vocabulary Review...................................... 354

Reteaching 355

Topic Assessment Practice 357

Topic Performance Task 359

TOPIC 9 in volume 2
Compare Two-Digit Numbers

enVision® STEM Project 361

Review What You Know.................................... 362

Pick a Project 363

3-ACT MATH Preview: Digit Flip 364

9-1 1 More, 1 Less; 10 More, 10 Less 365

9-2 Find Numbers on a Hundred Chart 369

9-3 Compare Numbers 373

9-4 Compare Numbers with Symbols (>, <, =)............... 377

9-5 Compare Numbers on a Number Line 381

9-6 PROBLEM SOLVING Make Sense and Persevere........... 385

Fluency Practice Activity................................. 389

Vocabulary Review...................................... 390

Reteaching 391

Topic Assessment Practice 393

Topic Performance Task 395

SavvasRealize.com

TOPIC 10 in volume 2
Use Models and Strategies to Add Tens and Ones

enVision® STEM Project 397
Review What You Know. 398
Pick a Project 399

10-1 Add Tens Using Models. 401

10-2 Mental Math: Ten More Than a Number 405

10-3 Add Tens and Ones Using a Hundred Chart 409

10-4 Add Tens and Ones Using an Open Number Line 413

10-5 Add Tens and Ones Using Models. 417

10-6 Make a Ten to Add. 421

10-7 Add Using Place Value 425

10-8 Practice Adding Using Strategies 429

10-9 PROBLEM SOLVING Model with Math 433

Fluency Practice Activity. 437
Vocabulary Review. 438
Reteaching 439
Topic Assessment Practice 443
Topic Performance Task 447

TOPIC 11 in volume 2
Use Models and Strategies to Subtract Tens

enVision® STEM Project 449
Review What You Know. 450
Pick a Project 451
3-ACT MATH Preview: So Many Colors. 452

11-1 Subtract Tens Using Models 453

11-2 Subtract Tens Using a Hundred Chart 457

11-3 Subtract Tens Using an Open Number Line 461

11-4 Use Addition to Subtract Tens. 465

11-5 Mental Math: Ten Less Than a Number 469

11-6 Use Strategies to Practice Subtraction 473

11-7 PROBLEM SOLVING Model with Math 477

Fluency Practice Activity. 481
Vocabulary Review. 482
Reteaching 483
Topic Assessment Practice 485
Topic Performance Task 487

TOPIC 12 in volume 2
Measure Lengths

enVision® STEM Project. 489
Review What You Know. 490
Pick a Project 491

12-1 Compare and Order by Length 493

12-2 Indirect Measurement 497

12-3 Use Units to Measure Length. 501

12-4 PROBLEM SOLVING Use Appropriate Tools 505

Fluency Practice Activity. 509
Vocabulary Review. 510
Reteaching 511
Topic Assessment Practice 513
Topic Performance Task 515

TOPIC 13 in volume 2
Time and Money

enVision® STEM Project. 517
Review What You Know. 518
Pick a Project 519
3-ACT MATH Preview: Drip Dry. 520

13-1 OPTIONAL Tell the Value of Coins. 521

13-2 OPTIONAL Find the Value of a Group of Coins 525

13-3 Understand the Hour and Minute Hands 529

13-4 Tell and Write Time to the Hour 533

13-5 Tell and Write Time to the Half Hour 537

13-6 PROBLEM SOLVING Reasoning 541

Fluency Practice Activity. 545
Vocabulary Review. 546
Reteaching 547
Topic Assessment Practice 549
Topic Performance Task 551

SavvasRealize.com

TOPIC 14 in volume 2
Reason with Shapes and Their Attributes

enVision® STEM Project. 553
Review What You Know. 554
Pick a Project 555

14-1 Use Attributes to Define Two-Dimensional (2-D) Shapes 557

14-2 Defining and Non-Defining Attributes of 2-D Shapes 561

14-3 Build and Draw 2-D Shapes by Attributes 565

14-4 Compose 2-D Shapes 569

14-5 Compose New 2-D Shapes from 2-D Shapes 573

14-6 Use Attributes to Define Three-Dimensional (3-D) Shapes 577

14-7 Defining and Non-Defining Attributes of 3-D Shapes 581

14-8 Compose with 3-D Shapes. 585

14-9 PROBLEM SOLVING Make Sense and Persevere. 589

Fluency Practice Activity. 593
Vocabulary Review. 594
Reteaching. 595
Topic Assessment Practice 599
Topic Performance Task 603

TOPIC 15 in volume 2
Equal Shares of Circles and Rectangles

enVision® STEM Project. 605
Review What You Know. 606
Pick a Project 607
3-ACT MATH Preview: Pieced Out 608

15-1 Make Equal Shares 609

15-2 Make Halves and Fourths of Rectangles and Circles. 613

15-3 Understand Halves and Fourths 617

15-4 PROBLEM SOLVING Model with Math 621

Fluency Practice Activity. 625
Vocabulary Review. 626
Reteaching. 627
Topic Assessment Practice 629
Topic Performance Task 631

Contents

Math Practices and Problem Solving Handbook

The **Math Practices and Problem Solving Handbook** is available at SavvasRealize.com.

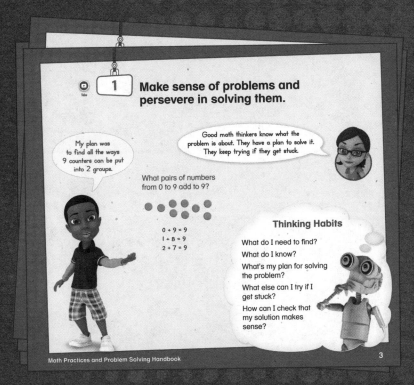

1 Make sense of problems and persevere in solving them.

My plan was to find all the ways 9 counters can be put into 2 groups.

Good math thinkers know what the problem is about. They have a plan to solve it. They keep trying if they get stuck.

What pairs of numbers from 0 to 9 add to 9?

$0 + 9 = 9$
$1 + 8 = 9$
$2 + 7 = 9$

Thinking Habits

What do I need to find?

What do I know?

What's my plan for solving the problem?

What else can I try if I get stuck?

How can I check that my solution makes sense?

Math Practices and Problem Solving Handbook 3

Math Practices

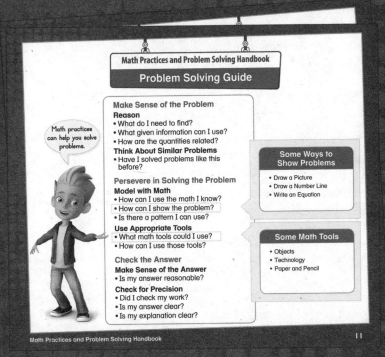

Math Practices and Problem Solving Handbook
Problem Solving Guide

Math practices can help you solve problems.

Make Sense of the Problem

Reason
- What do I need to find?
- What given information can I use?
- How are the quantities related?

Think About Similar Problems
- Have I solved problems like this before?

Persevere in Solving the Problem

Model with Math
- How can I use the math I know?
- How can I show the problem?
- Is there a pattern I can use?

Use Appropriate Tools
- What math tools could I use?
- How can I use those tools?

Check the Answer

Make Sense of the Answer
- Is my answer reasonable?

Check for Precision
- Did I check my work?
- Is my answer clear?
- Is my explanation clear?

Some Ways to Show Problems
- Draw a Picture
- Draw a Number Line
- Write an Equation

Some Math Tools
- Objects
- Technology
- Paper and Pencil

Math Practices and Problem Solving Handbook 11

Problem Solving Guide
Problem Solving Recording Sheet

Name _____

Writing Numbers 0 to 4

Practice writing the numbers 0–4.

1. 0 0 0

2. 1 1 1

3. 2 2 2

4. 3 3 3

5. 4 4 4

Writing Numbers 5 to 9

Practice writing the numbers 5–9.

1.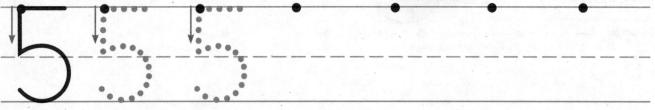

2.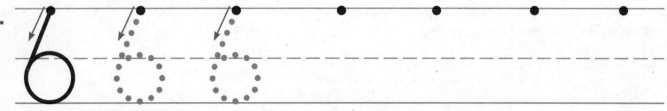

3.

4.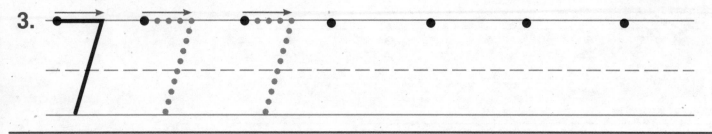

5.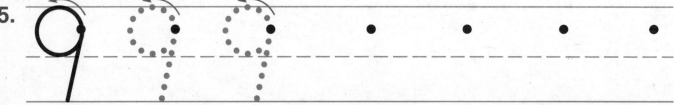

Grade 1 | Readiness

Name _____

Counting and Writing to 9

Count and write the number of dots.

1.  _____

2.  _____

3. _____

4.  _____

5.  _____

6. _____

7. _____

8.  _____

9. _____

Comparing Numbers Through 5

Write the number that tells how many.
Then circle the number that is less.

1.

2   **3**

2.

_____   _____

- - - - -   - - - - -

_____   _____

3.

_____   _____

- - - - -   - - - - -

_____   _____

4.

_____   _____

- - - - -   - - - - -

_____   _____

Grade 1 | Readiness

Name _____

Comparing Numbers Through 10

Write the number that tells how many.
Then circle the number that is greater.

1.

 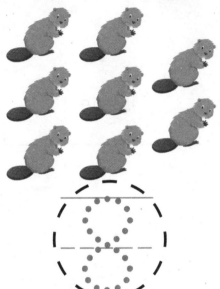

7   ⑧

2.

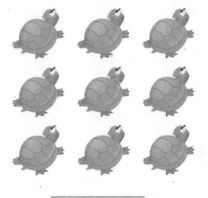 

_____   _____

– – – – –   – – – – –

_____   _____

Making Numbers 6 to 9

Write the number inside and outside.
Then write the number in all.

1.

_____ inside   _____ outside   _____ in all

2.

_____ inside   _____ outside   _____ in all

Write the numbers to show the parts.

3.

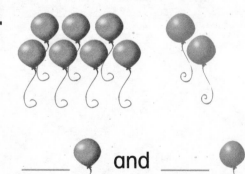

_____ and _____ 🎈

4.

_____ 🎈 and _____ 🎈

Grade 1 | Readiness

Name _____

Finding Missing Parts of Numbers 6 to 9

> Find the missing parts. Then write the numbers.

1. 6 bones in all.

_____   _____
part I know   missing part

2. 6 bones in all.

_____   _____
part I know   missing part

3. 7 bones in all.

_____   _____
part I know   missing part

4. 8

_____   _____
part I know   missing part

5. 9

_____   _____
part I know   missing part

6. 8

_____   _____
part I know   missing part

Find the missing part. Then complete the addition equation.

7. Mark has 9 bagels. He cooks 4 of them.
How many bagels are **NOT** cooked?

$4 + \underline{\quad} = 9$

8. Hanna has 7 eggs. 5 eggs hatched.
How many eggs are **NOT** hatched?

$5 + \underline{\quad} = 7$

Shapes

Color each shape below.

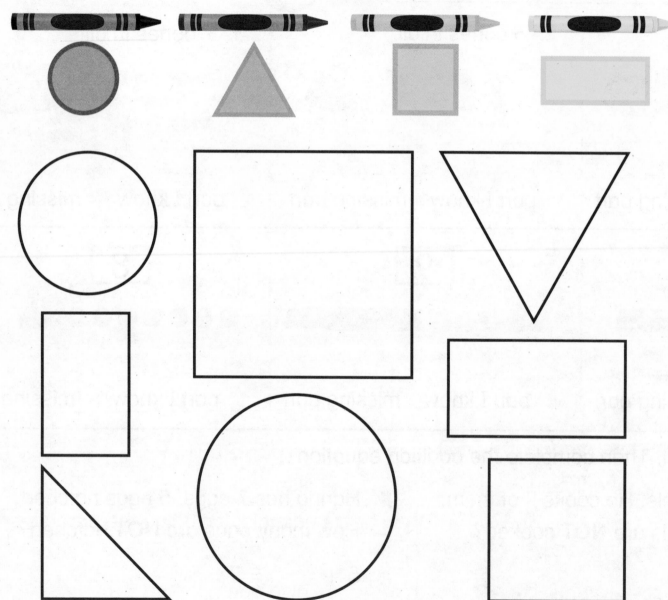

Grade I | Readiness

Understand Addition and Subtraction

Essential Question: What are ways to think about addition and subtraction?

Digital Resources

Interactive Student Edition   Activity   Visual Learning   Video   Practice

Assessment   Games   Tools   Glossary

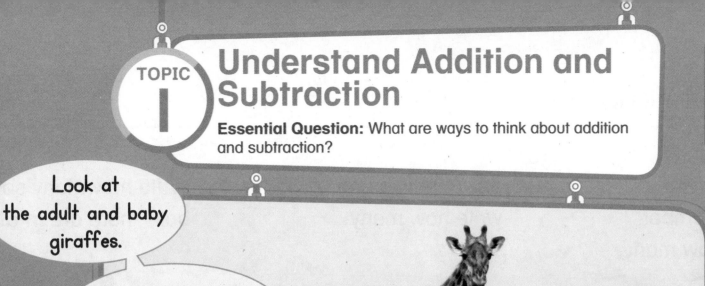

Look at the adult and baby giraffes.

How are they the same? How are they different?

Wow! Let's do this project and learn more.

enVision STEM Project: Parents and Babies

Find Out Talk to friends and relatives about different animals and their babies.
Ask them how the parents and babies are the same and how they are different.

Journal: Make a Book Show what you found. In your book, also:

• Draw some animals, including the parents and babies.

• Create and solve addition and subtraction stories about some animals and their babies.

Name _____

Review What You Know

Vocabulary

1. Count the fish. Write the number that tells how many.	**2. Join** the two groups and write how many.	**3.** Write how many soccer balls there are **in all**.

_____

_ _ _ _

_____

_ _ _ _

_____

_ _ _ _

Counting

4. Tammy has 4 balloons. Draw a picture of her balloons.

5. Write the number that tells how many cats.

_____

_ _ _ _

Sums

6. Circle the number that shows how many crabs you see.

2   3   4   5

Name _____

PROJECT
1A

Where do birds lay their eggs?

Project: Draw a Bird Clutch

PROJECT
1B

What is the most popular fruit juice in the world?

Project: Find Fruit Facts

PROJECT
1C

What are different homes made of?

Project: Build a Model

3-ACT MATH PREVIEW

Before watching the video, think:

What's your favorite snack to bring to school? How often do you pick your own snack? It's important to choose a snack that tastes good and is good for you.

I can ...
model with math to solve a problem that involves adding and subtracting.

Name _____

Solve & Share

4 dogs

Some dogs join.

How many dogs now?

Show how you solve.

_____ dogs now

5 cats

2 cats join.

How many cats now?

Use cubes.

I can use cubes to show cats.

Add 5 and 2.

5 + 2

plus

I can count to add.

Write the **sum**.

5 + 2 = 7

equals

There are 7 cats now.

Convince Me!

How do cubes help you solve the problem?

Guided Practice — Solve. Use cubes to help.

1. 3 cows

3 cows join.

How many cows now?

3 + 3 = 6 cows

2. 2 birds

6 birds join.

How many birds now?

___ ◯ ___ ◯ ___ birds

6 six

Name _____

Independent Practice ✩ Solve. Use cubes or draw a picture.

3. 4 bees   4 bees join.

How many bees now?

___ ◯ ___ ◯ ___ bees

4. 3 bugs   6 bugs join.

How many bugs now?

___ ◯ ___ ◯ ___ bugs

Solve the problem.
Draw a picture to help.

5. Higher Order Thinking

6 ducks

4 chickens

2 ducks join.

How many ducks in all?

_____ ducks in all

6.  **Vocabulary**

3 dogs

4 dogs join.

Add to find the **sum**.

____ ⬭ ____ ⬭ ____ dogs

7. Model

8 cats

1 cat joins.

How many cats now?

____ ⬭ ____ ⬭ ____ cats

8. Higher Order Thinking

Make up an addition story about the birds.

Use pictures, numbers, or words.

9. ☑ **Assessment Practice**

5 frogs   3 frogs join.

How many frogs now?

Ⓐ 5 + 1 = 6 frogs

Ⓑ 5 + 2 = 7 frogs

Ⓒ 5 + 3 = 8 frogs

Ⓓ 5 + 4 = 9 frogs

Solve & Share

4 red apples and 4 green apples
How many apples in all?

Show how you solve.

Use cubes to help.

Activity

Lesson 1-2
Put Together

I can ...
solve word problems about
putting parts together.

I can also reason
about math.

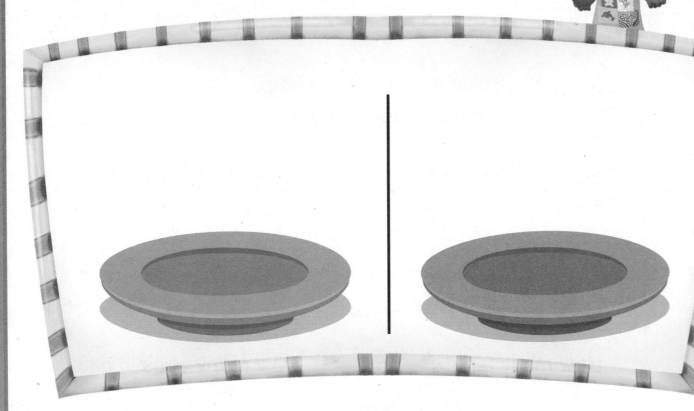

_____ apples in all

4 red fish and
2 blue fish

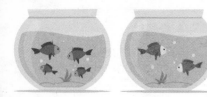

How many fish in all?

The **parts** are 4 and 2.

part   part

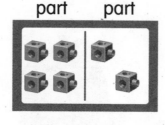

4   2

I can show fish on my mat.

Add the parts to find the **whole**.

4 + 2

The whole is also the sum.

Write an addition **equation**.

4 + 2 = 6

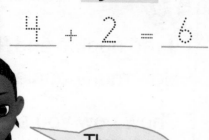

There are 6 fish in all.

Convince Me!

Use cubes.

Show 4 + 2.

Then show 2 + 4.

What do you notice?

☆ **Guided Practice** ☆   Solve. Use cubes to help.
Write an addition equation.

1. 3 yellow birds and
5 blue birds

How many birds in all?

3 + 5 = 8 birds

2. 1 white egg and
6 blue eggs

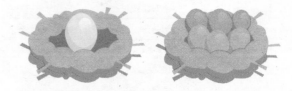

How many eggs in all?

____ ◯ ____ ◯ ____ eggs

Name _____

Independent Practice Solve. Use cubes or draw a picture.
Write an addition equation.

3. 3 little pigs and 4 big pigs

How many pigs in all?

___ ◯ ___ ◯ ___ pigs

4. 3 box cars and 3 tank cars

How many cars in all?

___ ◯ ___ ◯ ___ cars

5. Higher Order Thinking

2 red hats

3 shoes

7 blue hats

How many hats in all?

Draw a picture.

Write an addition equation.

___ ◯ ___ ◯ ___ hats

6. Make Sense

Jen has 2 red flowers
and 5 blue flowers.

How many flowers in all?

Write an equation.

Use cubes or draw
a picture.

_____ ◯ _____ ◯ _____ flowers

7. Higher Order Thinking

Write a picture story.
Show blue fish and green fish.
Write an addition equation.

Tell how many fish in all.

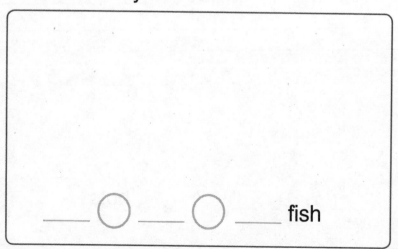

_____ ◯ _____ ◯ _____ fish

8. ☑ Assessment Practice

4 red apples and 5 green apples

How many apples in all?

Ⓐ $9 + 4 = 13$ apples

Ⓑ $4 + 5 = 9$ apples

Ⓒ $3 + 6 = 9$ apples

Ⓓ $4 + 4 = 8$ apples

Match the
parts and
the whole.

12 twelve

Solve & Share

Sarah has 5 pencils.
She puts some in the green cup.
She puts some in the red cup.

How many pencils could be in each cup?

Lesson 1-3

Both Addends Unknown

I can ...
solve problems by breaking the whole into parts.

I can also reason about math.

Show how you solve. Then talk to a partner. Are your answers the same?

7 penguins in all

Some are inside a cave.
Some are outside.

What are some ways?

Here is one way.

4 inside
3 outside

Write an equation.

7 = 4 + 3

whole   part   part

Here is another way.

7 = 5 + 2

5 inside
2 outside

Convince Me!

With 7 penguins, could 4 be inside the cave, and 4 be outside the cave?
Why or why not?

☆ **Guided Practice** ☆ How many penguins are inside and outside?
Use cubes or draw a picture.
Write an equation.

1. 5 penguins in all

5 = 3 + 2

2. 8 penguins in all

___ ◯ ___ ◯ ___

14   fourteen

Topic 1 | Lesson 3

Name _____

Independent Practice

How many bats are inside and outside?
Use cubes or draw a picture.
Write an equation.

3. 9 bats in all

___ ◯ ___ ◯ ___

4. 8 bats in all

___ ◯ ___ ◯ ___

5. 5 bats in all

___ ◯ ___ ◯ ___

6. 4 bats in all

___ ◯ ___ ◯ ___

7. enVision® STEM

8 monkeys in all
Some live in trees.
Some live on the ground.

Show one way.

_____ ⭘ _____ = _____ monkeys
in trees   on the
           ground

8. Reasoning

Anna draws 2 cats.

She draws 5 more cats.

How many cats in all?
Write an equation.

_____ ⭘ _____ = _____ cats

9. Higher Order Thinking

Andy has 10 balls.
1 or 2 balls are inside
the toy box.

How many balls are
outside the toy box?
Tell how you know.

Draw pictures.
Write equations.

10. ☑ Assessment Practice

9 birds in all
Some birds are flying.
Some birds are in a tree.

Which shows one way?

Ⓐ 4 flying, 3 in a tree

Ⓑ 5 flying, 4 in a tree

Ⓒ 1 flying, 7 in a tree

Ⓓ 8 flying, 2 in a tree

Topic 1 | Lesson 3

Name _____

Solve & Share

There are 6 ducks.

Some fly away.

How many ducks are left?

Show how you solve.

I can ...
solve word problems that
involve taking from a group.

I can also use math
tools correctly.

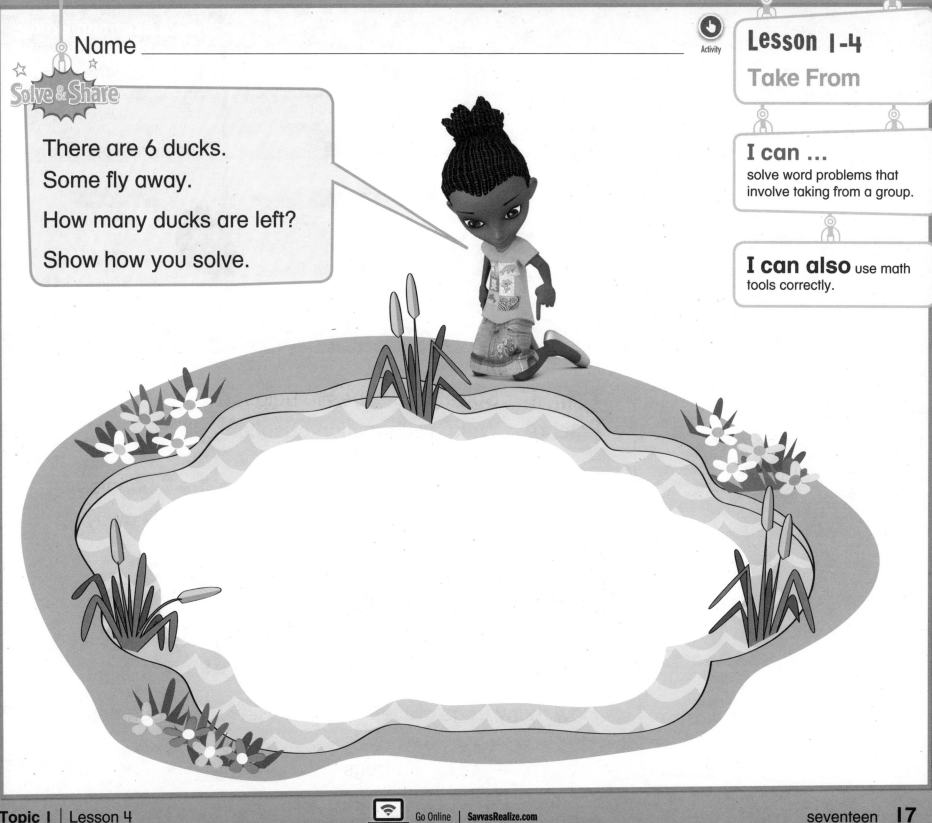

There are 7 ducks.
3 ducks fly away.

How many ducks are left?

Use cubes.

7

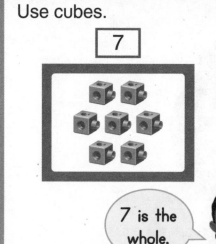

7 is the whole.

 **Subtract** 3 from 7.

7 - 3

minus

 →

3 ducks fly away.

Write the **difference.**

7 - 3 = 4

subtraction **equation**

There are 4 ducks left.

Convince Me!

How do cubes help you solve the problem?

☆ **Guided Practice** ☆   Solve. Use cubes to help.
Write a subtraction equation.

1. There are 6 frogs.
   2 frogs jump off.

How many frogs are left?

6 - 2 = 4 frogs

2. There are 7 bunnies.
   1 bunny hops away.

How many bunnies are left?

___ ◯ ___ ◯ ___ bunnies

Independent Practice Solve. Use cubes or draw a picture. Write a subtraction equation.

3. There are 8 bugs.
4 bugs fly away.

How many bugs are left?

____ ◯ ____ ◯ ____ bugs

4. There are 9 cats.
6 cats run away.

How many cats are left?

____ ◯ ____ ◯ ____ cats

5. Higher Order Thinking
There are 7 dogs.
Some run away.
3 dogs are left.

How many dogs ran away?

Draw a picture to help.

____ dogs

6. Reasoning

Lin has 9 stamps.

She gives away 4 stamps.

How many stamps are left?

____ ◯ ____ ◯ ____ stamps

7. Reasoning

Gloria has 8 flowers.

She gives away 5 flowers.

How many flowers are left?

____ ◯ ____ ◯ ____ flowers

8. Higher Order Thinking

Find the missing number.

Write a subtraction story for the equation.

$$7 - 2 = \underline{\quad}$$

_____

_____

_____

_____

9. ☑ Assessment Practice

There are 8 bees.

6 bees fly away.

How many bees are left?

Ⓐ $8 - 2 = 6$ bees

Ⓑ $8 - 7 = 1$ bees

Ⓒ $7 - 2 = 5$ bees

Ⓓ $8 - 6 = 2$ bees

Name _____

Solve & Share

There are 5 red cars and 3 blue cars.
Are there more red cars or blue cars?
How many more?

Show how you know.

I can ...
solve word problems that involve how many more.

I can also reason about math.

5 blue hats
2 orange hats

How many **more** blue hats
than orange hats are there?

Use cubes to **compare**.

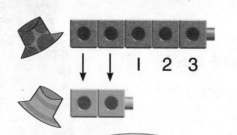

You can also write
an equation
to compare.

One way is to find the difference.
Write a subtraction equation.

$$5 - 2 = 3$$

There are 3 more
blue hats than
orange hats.

Convince Me!

Can you also add to
solve the problem above?
Explain.

☆ **Guided Practice** ☆ Use cubes to help.
Write an equation. Then solve.

1. 6 yellow frogs
   3 green frogs

How many more yellow frogs than green frogs are there?

$$6 - 3 = 3$$

_____ more yellow frogs

Name _____

Independent Practice Use cubes or draw a picture.
Write an equation. Then solve.

2. 3 brown dogs

I black dog

How many more brown dogs than
black dogs are there?

___ ◯ ___ ◯ ___

____ more brown dogs

3. 7 red beads

4 green beads

How many more red beads than green
beads are there?

___ ◯ ___ ◯ ___

____ more red beads

Higher Order Thinking
There are more blue birds than yellow birds.
Write 2 equations to show. Then solve.

You can use
cubes to help.

4.

____ – ____ = ____

____ + ____ = ____

____ more blue birds

5. Number Sense

4 fish are in a tank.

2 fish are sold.

How many fish are left?

____ ◯ ____ ◯ ____

____ fish

6. Model

Luis sees 5 green frogs.

He sees 1 blue frog.

How many more green frogs than blue frogs does Luis see?

____ ◯ ____ ◯ ____

____ more green frogs

7. Higher Order Thinking

Draw some yellow flowers.
Draw more red flowers than yellow flowers.

How many more red flowers than yellow flowers are there?

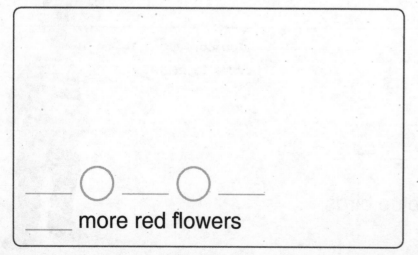

____ ◯ ____ ◯ ____

____ more red flowers

8. ☑ Assessment Practice

6 gray cats

4 white cats

How many more gray cats than white cats are there?

Ⓐ 2 more gray cats

Ⓑ 4 more gray cats

Ⓒ 6 more gray cats

Ⓓ 10 more gray cats

Draw a picture or use cubes to help.

Name _____

Solve & Share

Amy has 7 stickers.
Tim has 5 stickers.

Who has fewer stickers?
How many fewer?

Show how you know.

I can ...
solve word problems that involve how many fewer.

I can also use repeated reasoning.

Troy has 5 red cars.
Barb has 9 green cars.

 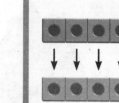

How many **fewer** cars does Troy have than Barb?

5 is less than 9. Troy has fewer cars.

Use cubes to compare.

1 2 3 4

You can subtract to compare. Troy has 4 fewer cars.

$$\underline{9} - \underline{5} = \underline{4}$$

Convince Me!

How is finding how many fewer like finding how many more?

☆ **Guided Practice** ☆ Use cubes to help.
Write an equation. Then solve.

1. Juan has 8 red crayons.
   Sue has 2 blue crayons.

   How many fewer crayons does Sue have than Juan?

   $$\underline{8} - \underline{2} = \underline{6}$$

   $\underline{6}$ fewer crayons

2. Ann has 4 purple grapes.
   Sam has 7 green grapes.

   How many fewer grapes does Ann have than Sam?

   $\underline{} \bigcirc \underline{} \bigcirc \underline{}$

   ___ fewer grapes

Tools   Assessment

Independent Practice Use cubes or draw a picture.
Write an equation. Then solve.

3. Emma buys 10 red apples.
   She buys 5 green apples.

   How many fewer green apples than
   red apples does Emma buy?

   ___ ◯ ___ ◯ ___

   ____ fewer green apples

4. Beth writes on 3 cards.
   Joe writes on 9 cards.

   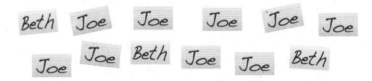

   How many fewer cards does
   Beth write on than Joe?

   ___ ◯ ___ ◯ ___

   ____ fewer cards

5. **Higher Order Thinking**

   There are fewer white kites than blue kites.
   Write 2 equations to show. Then solve.

   ___ − ___ = ___

   ___ + ___ = ___

   ____ fewer white kites

   Both equations
   use the same
   numbers.

6. Reasoning Leah has 3 pens.

Scott has 6 pens.

How many pens do they have in all?

___ ◯ ___ ◯ ___

____ pens

7. Reasoning

There are 7 oranges on a branch.

3 oranges fall off.

How many oranges are left?

___ ◯ ___ ◯ ___ |

____ oranges

8. Higher Order Thinking

Draw some blue balloons.

Draw fewer yellow balloons.

How many fewer yellow balloons than blue balloons are there?

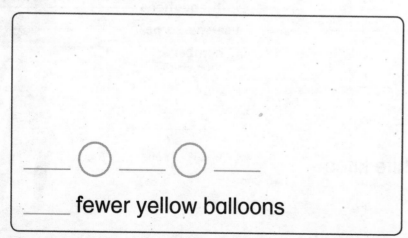

___ ◯ ___ ◯ ___

____ fewer yellow balloons

9. ☑ Assessment Practice

8 apple trees

6 pear trees

How many fewer pear trees than apple trees are there?

Ⓐ 2 fewer pear trees

Ⓑ 3 fewer pear trees

Ⓒ 6 fewer pear trees

Ⓓ 8 fewer pear trees

Name _____

 **Solve & Share**

There are 5 train cars.

More train cars join.

Now there are 9 train cars.

How many train cars joined?

I can ...
use addition or subtraction to help find a missing addend.

I can also make sense of problems.

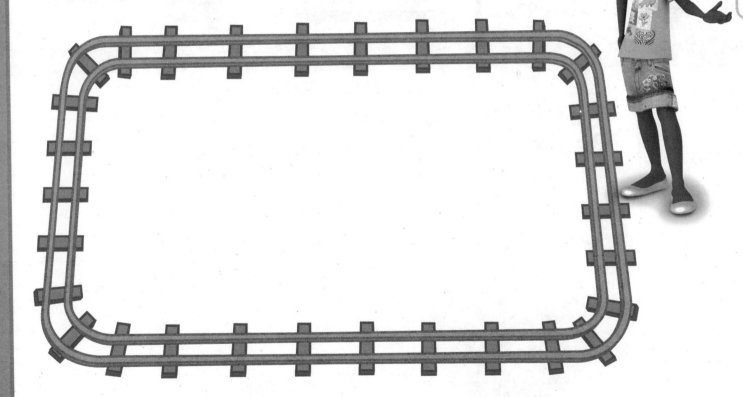

_____ train cars joined.

A station has 7 train cars.

More cars come in.
Now there are 9 cars.
How many cars came in?

Use cubes.

9

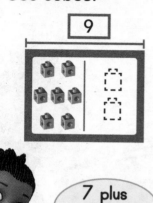

7 plus what is 9?

Find the missing **addend**.
Make a model.

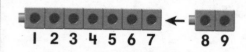
1 2 3 4 5 6 7   8 9

7 and 2 more make 9.

Write an addition equation.

$$7 + 2 = 9$$
addends   sum

2 more cars came in.

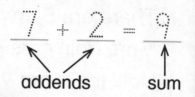

Convince Me!

Can you also subtract to solve the problem above? Explain.

☆ Guided ☆ Practice Use cubes to help. Write an equation. Then solve.

1. Bobby has 4 fish.

He buys more fish.
Now he has 7 fish.

How many fish did Bobby buy?

$$4 + 3 = 7$$

____ fish

Name _____

Independent Practice   Use cubes or draw a picture.
Write an equation. Then solve.

2. Mary has 4 stickers.

Pat gives her more stickers.

Now Mary has 8 stickers.

How many stickers did Pat give Mary?

___ ◯ ___ ◯ ___

____ stickers

3. Billy draws 4 red cars.

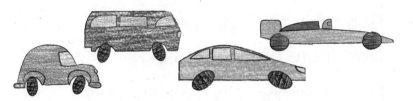

Then he draws some blue cars.

Now there are 10 cars.

How many blue cars did Billy draw?

___ ◯ ___ ◯ ___

____ blue cars

4. Higher Order Thinking

Some girls are on the bus.

2 boys get on the bus.

Now there are 7 children on the bus.

How many girls are on the bus?

Write 2 equations to show.

Then solve.

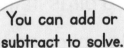
You can add or subtract to solve.

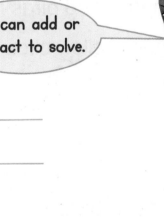

____ + ____ = ____

____ − ____ = ____

____ girls

5. 6 pencils are on the desk.

Bob adds more pencils.

Now there are 9 pencils.

How many pencils did Bob add?

_____ pencils

6. Use Tools

Nora has 3 pretzels and 7 crackers.

How many snacks does she have in all?

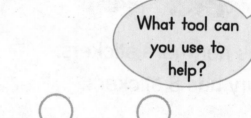

What tool can you use to help?

_____ ◯ _____ ◯ _____

_____ snacks

7. Higher Order Thinking

Some yellow birds are in a tree.

Some blue birds join them.

Now there are 5 birds in the tree.

How many yellow birds and blue birds could there be?

_____ yellow birds and _____ blue birds

8. ☑ Assessment Practice

4 puppies play.

More puppies join them.

Now there are 7 puppies.

How many puppies joined?

Ⓐ 5 puppies

Ⓑ 4 puppies

Ⓒ 3 puppies

Ⓓ 2 puppies

Practice Adding and Subtracting

Name _____

Solve & Share

5 pebbles are brown.

The other pebbles are black.

There are 7 pebbles in all.

How many black pebbles are there?

I can ...
solve word problems that involve putting together or taking apart.

I can also model with math.

_____ black pebbles

8 students are in a class.

5 of the students are boys.

How many of the students are girls?

You can make a model.

Think about the whole. Show the part you know.

8

?

Find the missing part.

You know how to **add** to find the missing part.

8

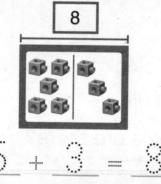

$5 + 3 = 8$

3 students are girls.

You can also **subtract** to find the missing part.

8

$8 - 5 = 3$

3 students are girls.

Convince Me!

Compare the addition and subtraction equations. What do you notice about the numbers?

☆ **Guided Practice** ☆

Use cubes to help.
Write an equation. Then solve.

1. Nick has 9 robots.

   3 of the robots can talk.

   eep eep · hi there · bobo bobo

   How many robots cannot talk?

   $3 + \underline{\quad} = 9$

   _____ robots

2. 6 children play at the beach.

   2 children are girls.

   How many are boys?

   $\underline{\quad} \underline{\quad} \underline{\quad} \bigcirc \underline{\quad}$

   _____ boys

Name _____

Independent Practice Use cubes or draw a picture.
Write an equation. Then solve.

3. Jill has 9 cards.

5 cards are soccer cards.

The rest are baseball cards.

How many baseball cards are there?

_____ baseball cards

4. Rita has 7 shells.

3 shells are big.

The rest are small.

How many small shells does Rita have?

_____ small shells

5. Higher Order Thinking

Henry has 6 candles on his cake.

I candle is green.

The rest are blue.

How many blue candles are there?

Write 2 equations to show. Then solve.

You can think addition to subtract.

____ + ____ = ____

____ − ____ = ____

_____ blue candles

6. Make Sense

Joe buys 2 red fish.

He buys some blue fish.

He buys 9 fish in all.

How many blue fish does Joe buy?

____ blue fish

7. Make Sense

Rachel has 8 nickels.

She gives away 4 nickels.

How many nickels are left?

____ nickels

8. Higher Order Thinking

Nina has 8 stuffed animals.

Some are bears.

Some are tigers.

How many of each animal
could Nina have?

____ bears and ____ tigers

9. ☑ Assessment Practice

Liz and Mary have 7 fish in all.

Liz has 2 fish.

How many fish does Mary have?

Which equation matches the story?

Ⓐ 9 − 2 = 7 fish

Ⓑ 7 − 1 = 6 fish

Ⓒ 7 − 2 = 5 fish

Ⓓ 8 − 7 = 1 fish

Use cubes
to help.

Name _____

Solve & Share

Do you add or subtract to solve the problem?
Tell why. Show how to solve.
Use pictures, numbers, or words.

Problem Solving

Lesson 1-9
Construct Arguments

I can ...
construct math arguments using addition and subtraction.

I can also add and subtract to 10.

7 rabbits

3 turtles

How many more rabbits than turtles?

Thinking Habits

How can I use math to explain my work?

Is my explanation clear?

This box has 9 crayons in all.

CRAYONS

6 crayons are blue.

The rest are red.

How many are red?

Solve and explain.

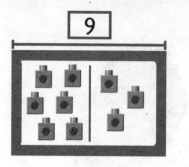
9

6 + 3 = 9

3

I used cubes. I counted.

6   3

9 − 6 = 3

3 red

I made a picture. I used numbers.

Convince Me!

Look at the two ways to find the number of red crayons. How are the ways alike? How are the ways different?

☆ **Guided Practice** ☆ Solve. Use pictures, numbers, or words to explain.

1. Manny draws 6 tiles.

   4 tiles are red.

   The others are green.

   How many green tiles does Manny draw?

   :····::····::····::····:   :····::····:

Tools Assessment

Independent Practice ☆ Solve. Use pictures, numbers, or words to explain.

2. Jan has 8 pennies.
She spends 5 pennies.

How many pennies does Jan have left?

3. Lidia has 7 pencils.
Jon has 2 pencils.

Who has fewer pencils?
How many fewer?

4. Higher Order Thinking

Max has 3 apples.
He buys 2 more apples.
He gives away 4 apples.

How many apples does Max have left?
Explain.

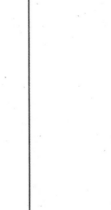

Problem Solving

Lemonade Stand

Some friends sell lemonade.

Solve each problem.

Use pictures, numbers, or words to explain.

5. Explain

Alex sells 3 cups.
Mark sells 5 cups.
How many cups do they sell in all?

Here is Alex's work.

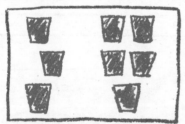

3+5=8 cups

Is his work correct? Tell why.

6. Be Precise

Mia sells 2 cups.
Gina sells 6 cups.

How many more cups does Gina sell than Mia?

Show the Word

Color these sums and differences. Leave the rest white.

| 4 | 3 | 5 |

I can ...
add and subtract within 5.

I can also be precise in my work.

8 – 3	0 + 1	0 + 5	5 – 2	3 + 0	5 – 2	5 – 1	2 + 2	3 + 1
2 + 3	0 + 2	7 – 2	1 + 2	0 + 2	4 – 1	1 – 1	4 – 0	5 – 5
10 – 5	5 + 0	3 + 2	3 + 0	5 – 2	3 – 0	0 + 1	1 + 3	5 – 4
4 + 1	5 – 4	5 – 0	4 – 1	4 – 4	2 + 1	2 + 0	4 + 0	0 + 1
9 – 4	1 + 1	1 + 4	3 – 0	4 – 3	0 + 3	3 – 2	0 + 4	3 – 1

The word is

_____ _____ _____

Glossary

Word List

- add
- addend
- compare
- difference
- equals (=)
- equation
- fewer
- minus (−)
- more
- part
- plus (+)
- subtract
- sum
- whole

Understand Vocabulary

1. Write an addition equation.

___ ◯ ___ ◯ ___

2. Write a subtraction equation.

___ ◯ ___ ◯ ___

3. Circle the difference.

$$8 - 2 = 6$$

4. Circle one part.

$$5 + 3 = 8$$

5. Circle the plus sign.

$$3 + 4 = 7$$

Use Vocabulary in Writing

6. Tell how to find $8 - 4$.
   Use at least one word from
   the Word List.

Name _____

Set A _____

You can solve problems about adding to.

3 turtles
1 more joins.

How many turtles now?

$$\underline{3} + \underline{1} = \underline{4} \text{ turtles}$$

plus   equals

Solve. Use cubes or draw a picture.

1. 5 flowers
2 more flowers

How many flowers now?

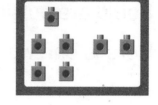

____ ◯ ____ ◯ ____ flowers

Set B _____

You can solve problems about putting together.

3 red markers and 2 blue markers

How many markers in all?

part   part

$$\underline{3} + \underline{2} = \underline{5} \text{ markers}$$

Solve. Use cubes or draw a picture.

2. 4 red cars and 2 blue cars

How many cars in all?

____ ◯ ____ ◯ ____ cars

You can solve problems with both addends unknown.

7 penguins in all
Some are inside a cave.
Some are outside.

Here is one way.

$\underline{7} = \underline{2} + \underline{5}$
whole   part   part

Use cubes or draw a picture.
Write an equation to solve.

3. 6 penguins in all
   Some are inside.
   Some are outside.
   Show one way.

___ ◯ ___ ◯ ___

4. 9 penguins in all
   Some are inside.
   Some are outside.
   Show one way.

___ = ___ ◯ ___

You can solve problems about taking from.

There are 6 pears.
Mia takes 3 pears away.

How many pears are left?

$\underline{6} - \underline{3} = \underline{3}$ pears

Use cubes or draw a picture.
Write an equation and solve.

5. There are 7 carrots.
   3 carrots are picked.

   How many carrots are left?

___ ◯ ___ ◯ ___ carrots

Name _____

Set E _____

You can solve problems about comparing.

4 blue pens
3 yellow pens
How many more blue pens than yellow pens are there?

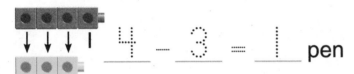 4 − 3 = 1 pen

Use cubes or draw a picture.
Write an equation and solve.

6. 4 black pens and 1 red pen
   How many more black pens than red pens?

   ___ ◯ ___ ◯ ___ more black pens

7. 3 baseballs and 7 soccer balls
   How many fewer baseballs than soccer balls?

   ___ ◯ ___ ◯ ___ fewer baseballs

Set F _____

You can find a missing addend to solve problems.

Ty has 4 grapes.
He takes some more grapes.
Now he has 9 grapes.

How many grapes did Ty take?

Ty took 5 grapes.

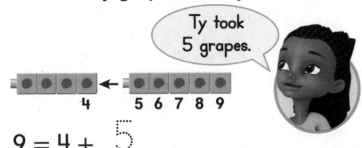

9 = 4 + 5

Use cubes or draw a picture.
Write an equation and solve.

8. Ivy has 2 fish in a bowl.
   She adds some more fish.
   Now Ivy has 5 fish.

   How many fish did she add?

   ___ ◯ ___ ◯ ___ ___ fish

You can add or subtract to find a missing part.

Tom has 9 shirts.

He has 4 red shirts.

The rest are blue.

How many blue shirts does Tom have?

Add: 4 + __5__ = 9

Or subtract: 9 − 4 = __5__

__5__ blue shirts

Use cubes or draw a picture.
Write an equation and solve.

9. Gigi has 8 pairs of shoes.

4 pairs are tennis shoes.

The rest are sandals.

How many pairs are sandals?

___ ◯ ___ ◯ ___

___ pairs of sandals

Thinking Habits

Construct Arguments

How can I use math to explain my work?

Is my explanation clear?

Solve. Use pictures, numbers, or words to explain.

10. Luc has 8 fish.

He gives away 4 fish.

How many fish does Luc have left?

Name _____

1. There are 8 penguins.
Some go inside the cave.
Some stay outside.

Match the number of penguins
inside the cave with the number
of penguins outside.

| **Inside:** | 5 penguins | 4 penguins | 7 penguins |

| **Outside:** | 1 penguin | 3 penguins | 4 penguins |

2. Sage had 10 peppers.
She cooks 3 of them.
How many peppers are left?

Write a subtraction equation to solve.

_____ ◯ _____ ◯ _____ peppers

3. Sara has 5 green beads and 3 red beads.
How many beads does she have in all?

Write an addition equation to solve.

_____ ◯ _____ ◯ _____ beads

4. Trina has 9 markers.
   Then she gives 5 markers to David.

   Which equation shows how many
   markers Trina has left?

   Ⓐ $7 - 2 = 5$

   Ⓑ $7 - 3 = 4$

   Ⓒ $9 - 5 = 4$

   Ⓓ $9 - 3 = 6$

5. George had 7 postcards.
   Then he gets some more.
   Now he has 9 postcards.

   Which equation does NOT describe
   the story?

   Ⓐ $7 + 2 = 9$

   Ⓑ $6 + 3 = 9$

   Ⓒ $9 - 7 = 2$

   Ⓓ $9 - 2 = 7$

6. Dante has 5 books. He wants to have 7 books.
   How many more books does Dante need to have 7 in all?

   7 books   5 books   4 books   2 books

   Ⓐ   Ⓑ   Ⓒ   Ⓓ

7. Lucy and Ellie have 6 cubes in all.
Ellie has 5 cubes.
How many cubes does Lucy have?

Choose three equations that show the story.

$6 - 4 = 2$ ☐ $6 - 5 = 1$ ☐ $5 + 1 = 6$ ☐ $3 + 3 = 6$ ☐ $6 - 1 = 5$ ☐

8. Trina has 6 ribbons. Julie has 2 ribbons.
What could happen for them to have the same number of ribbons?

Ⓐ Julie gives 1 of her ribbons to Trina.

Ⓑ Trina gives 1 of her ribbons to Julie.

Ⓒ Trina gives 2 of her ribbons to Julie.

Ⓓ Trina gives 4 of her ribbons to Julie.

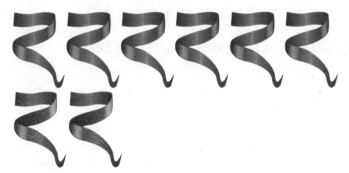

9. Draw the missing cubes on the mat.
Then write a subtraction equation that shows the story.

Owen has 5 blocks. He gives 1 to Jordan.
How many blocks does Owen have left?

____ ◯ ____ ◯ ____ blocks

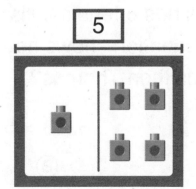

5

10. Hannah has 9 flowers. Carrie has 6 flowers. Which equation shows how many fewer flowers Carrie has than Hannah?

$9 - 9 = 0$ $9 - 6 = 3$ $9 + 1 = 10$ $9 + 2 = 11$

  Ⓐ   Ⓑ   Ⓒ   Ⓓ

---

11. Laura has 7 pears.

She wants to keep 2 pears for herself and give one to each of 6 friends.

Will Laura have enough pears?
Use pictures and words to explain.

---

12. Nikki has 8 tennis balls.
Thomas has 6 tennis balls.
Which equation shows how many more tennis balls Nikki has than Thomas?

$5 + 3 = 8$ $8 - 3 = 5$ $2 - 0 = 2$ $8 - 6 = 2$

  Ⓐ   Ⓑ   Ⓒ   Ⓓ

Name _____

Skating Ribbons

Marta is an ice skater.

She wins ribbons for her skating.

1. Marta wins 2 blue ribbons.
   She wins 4 red ribbons.

   How many ribbons does she win in all?

   _____ ribbons

2. Marta has 4 red ribbons.
   She wins some more red ribbons.
   Now she has 7 red ribbons.

   How many more red ribbons did Marta win?

   _____ more red ribbons

   Write an equation to show why your answer is correct.

   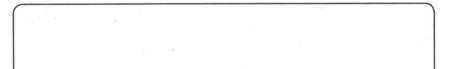

3. Marta has 8 yellow ribbons.
She put some on her door.
She puts the rest on her wall.

Write two different addition equations to show two ways she can put the ribbons on her door or on her wall.

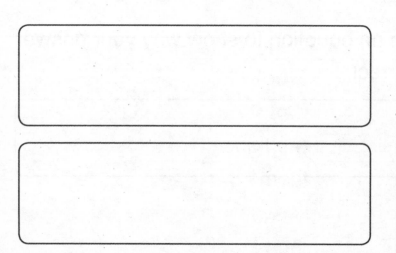

4. Marta has 8 yellow ribbons.
She has 2 blue ribbons.

How many more yellow ribbons than blue ribbons does Marta have?

_____ more yellow ribbons

5. Explain why your answer to Item 4 is correct. Use numbers, pictures, or words.

Fluently Add and Subtract Within 10

Essential Question: What strategies can you use while adding and subtracting?

Digital Resources

Interactive Student Edition | Activity | Visual Learning | Video | Practice

Assessment | Games | Tools | Glossary

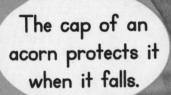

The cap of an acorn protects it when it falls.

What could people wear to protect themselves from a fall?

Wow! Let's do this project and learn more.

ēnVision STEM Project: Protect Yourself

Find Out Think of things that help plants and animals survive. What helps humans survive? Do we make things to help protect us?

Journal: Make a Book Show what you found out. In your book, also:

- Make a list of some things that humans make to protect themselves.

- Make up and solve addition and subtraction problems about these things.

Name _____

Review What You Know

A-Z Vocabulary

1. Circle the numbers that are the **parts**.

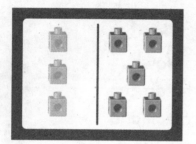

$$3 + 5 = 8$$

2. Circle the number that is the **whole**.

$$3 + 5 = 8$$

3. Circle the symbol for **equals**.

$$+ \quad - \quad =$$

Understanding Addition

4. Write an addition equation to match the picture.

____ + ____ = ____

5. Bob sees 5 bees. Ella sees some bees. They see 9 bees in all. How many bees did Ella see?

Write an addition equation to solve.

____ + ____ = ____

Making Numbers

6. Draw counters to show one way to make 8.

Name _____

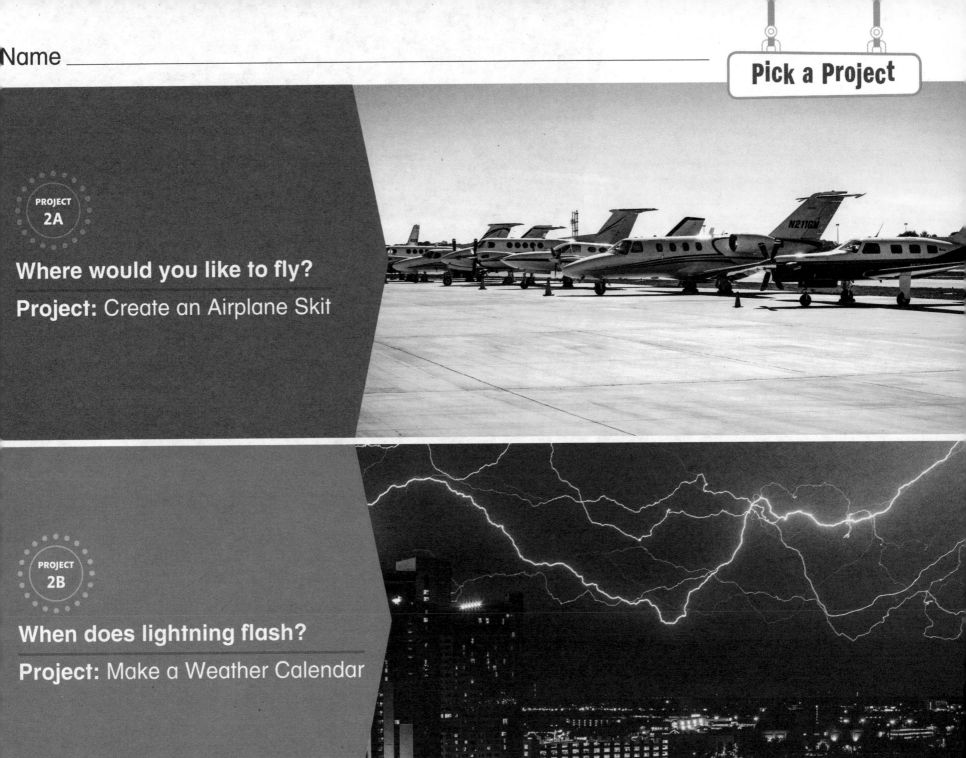

PROJECT 2A

Where would you like to fly?

Project: Create an Airplane Skit

PROJECT 2B

When does lightning flash?

Project: Make a Weather Calendar

Would you like to travel in space?

Project: Draw a Space Travel Picture

Are these apes or monkeys?

Project: Make a Poster of Apes and Monkeys

Activity

Solve & Share

You give the rabbit a number card. The rabbit puts that many carrots in the pot. Then he puts 2 more carrots in the pot.

How can you find how many carrots are in the pot without counting all the carrots?

I can ...
add by counting on from a number.

I can also model with math.

There are 4 tomatoes in the pot.
Add 2 more.
How many tomatoes are in the pot now?

You can use a **number line**.
Count on to find the sum.

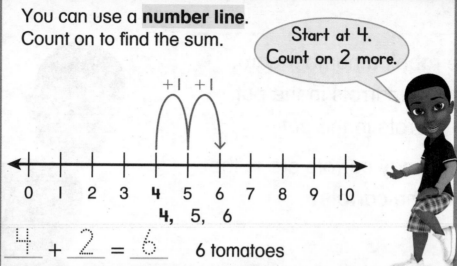

Start at 4.
Count on 2 more.

4, 5, 6

$4 + 2 = 6$ 6 tomatoes

You can add to join the two groups.

$4 + 2 = 6$

2 more than 4 is 6. There are 6 tomatoes in the pot!

Convince Me! How do you add 1 to any number? How do you add 2 to any number?

⭐ **Guided Practice**   Count on to find the sum.

1.

$3 + 2 = 5$

2.

___ + ___ = ___

3.

___ + ___ = ___

4.

___ + ___ = ___

Independent Practice ☆   Count on to add.

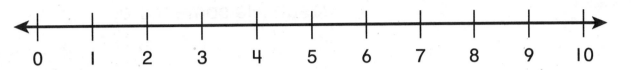

You can use a number line to help.

5. 2 + 3 = _____

6. 8 + 1 = _____

7. 7 + 1 = _____

8. 9 + 1 = _____

9. 4 + 3 = _____

10. 9 = 6 + _____

11. 2 + 6 = _____

12. 6 = 5 + _____

13. 5 + 3 = _____

14. Number Sense Circle **True** or **False**. Count on to help you.

8 + 0 = 8	True	False	3 + 1 = 5	True	False
7 + 1 = 7	True	False	6 = 4 + 0	True	False
8 = 6 + 2	True	False	6 + 1 = 7	True	False

15. Model

Dana has 7 grapes.

She gets 3 more.

How many grapes now?

____ ◯ ____ = ____

Dana has ____ grapes.

16. Model

Anna fills 6 bowls.

Jason fills some more.

Now there are 9 bowls filled.

How many bowls did Jason fill?

____ ◯ ____ = ____

Jason filled ____ bowls.

17. Higher Order Thinking

Max has 1 more carrot than Jena.

Jena has 3 more carrots than Sal.

Sal has 4 carrots.

Write how many carrots each person has.

____   ____   ____

Max   Jena   Sal

18. ☑ **Assessment Practice**

Which is the sum for 5 + 2?

Ⓐ 3

Ⓑ 6

Ⓒ 7

Ⓓ 8

You can count on to help add.

Name _____

Solve & Share

Emily and I have the same number of toys.
How many toys could each of us have?
How many toys do we have in all?

You can use cubes to help.

I can ...
use doubles to solve problems.

I can also look for things that repeat.

This is a **doubles fact**.

$$2 + 2 = 4$$

The addends are the same.

Every cube has a partner.

$$\begin{array}{r} 2 \\ + 2 \\ \hline 4 \end{array}$$

This is not a doubles fact. Every cube does not have a partner.

$$2 + 1 = 3$$

The addends are not the same.

Think of doubles when both addends are the same.

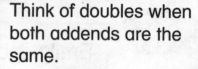

$$\begin{array}{r} 2 \\ + 2 \\ \hline 4 \end{array}$$

$$\begin{array}{r} 1 \\ + 1 \\ \hline 2 \end{array}$$

Convince Me! Is 6 + 4 a double? Explain.

☆**Guided Practice** Write the sum for each double.

1.

$$\underline{4} + \underline{4} = \underline{8}$$

2.

$$\underline{} + \underline{} = \underline{}$$

3.

$$\underline{} = \underline{} + \underline{}$$

4.

$$\underline{} + \underline{} = \underline{}$$

Topic 2 | Lesson 2

Independent Practice ☆   Write the sum for each doubles fact.

5.

___ + ___ = ___

6.

___ + ___ = ___

7.

___ + ___ = ___

8. 2
   + 2
   ☐

9. 4
   + 4
   ☐

10. 0
    + 0
    ☐

11. (A-Z) **Vocabulary**

Draw a picture to show a **doubles fact**.

Then write the addition equation to match.

___ + ___ = ___

12. Make Sense

Neela makes 4 pies.

John makes the same number of pies.

How many pies do they make in all?

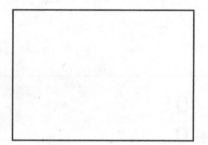 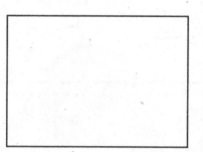

_____ pies

13. Make Sense

Kim has 2 pockets.

She has 5 dimes in each pocket.

How many dimes does Kim have in all?

 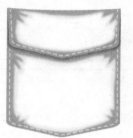

_____ dimes

14. Higher Order Thinking

Can a doubles fact have a sum of 9?
Draw a picture to find out.
Circle **Yes** or **No**.

Yes   **No**

15. ☑ Assessment Practice

Which doubles fact has a sum of 6?

Ⓐ 2 + 2

Ⓑ 3 + 2

Ⓒ 3 + 3

Ⓓ 4 + 4

Activity

Solve & Share

Look at these addition problems.

$3 + 3$ $2 + 2$ $4 + 5$ $3 + 4$ $2 + 3$ $4 + 4$

How are they alike? How are they different?

Sort them into two groups and write them in the buckets.

I can …
solve problems using near doubles facts.

I can also reason about math.

You can use a doubles fact to find a **near doubles fact**.

$4 + 5 = ?$
$4 + 6 = ?$

I can use the doubles fact $4 + 4$.

$4 + 5$ is $4 + 4$ and 1 more.

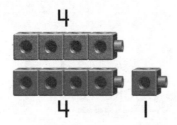

4

4   1

8 and 1 more is 9.

$4 + 6$ is $4 + 4$ and 2 more.

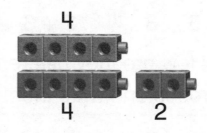

4

4   2

8 and 2 more is 10.

$$\begin{array}{r} 4 \\ +5 \\ \hline 9 \end{array} \qquad \begin{array}{r} 4 \\ +6 \\ \hline 10 \end{array}$$

Knowing doubles facts can help find near doubles facts.

Convince Me! How does knowing $3 + 3$ help you find $3 + 4$?

☆ **Guided Practice** ☆ Use a doubles fact to find each near doubles fact.

1. $2 + 3 = ?$

$\underline{2} + \underline{2} = \underline{4}$

So, $\underline{2} + \underline{3} = \underline{5}$.

2. $2 + 4 = ?$

$\underline{} + \underline{} = \underline{}$

So, $\underline{} + \underline{} = \underline{}$.

Independent Practice   Use a doubles fact to find each near doubles fact.

3. 3 + 4 = ?

___ + ___ = ___

So, ___ + ___ = ___ .

4. 3 + 5 = ?

___ + ___ = ___

So, ___ + ___ = ___ .

5.   4
   + 5
   ☐

6.   2
   + 4
   ☐

7.   2
   + 1
   ☐

8. 3 + 2 = ___

9. 1 + 3 = ___

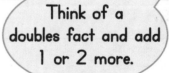

Think of a doubles fact and add 1 or 2 more.

Number Sense Write the missing numbers.

10. If 2 + ___ = 4, then 2 + ___ = 5.

11. If 4 + ___ = 8, then 4 + ___ = 9.

12. Reasoning

Omar eats 2 pears.

Jane eats 2 pears and then 2 more.

How many pears do Omar and Jane eat in all?

_____ pears in all

13. Reasoning

Sam finds 3 shells.

Jack finds 4 shells.

How many shells do they find in all?

_____ shells in all

14. Higher Order Thinking

Use a near doubles fact.

Write a story that uses that fact.

You can use pictures, words, and numbers.

15. ☑ **Assessment Practice**

Add $4 + 3$.

Ⓐ 10

Ⓑ 9

Ⓒ 8

Ⓓ 7

You can use a doubles fact to help.

Name _____

Solve & Share

Take a small handful of counters.
Toss them onto the page.
Place them on the ten-frame.
Write an addition equation to match the red and yellow counters.
Tell how a ten-frame helps you add.

I can ...
use a ten-frame to help solve addition facts with 5 and 10.

I can also model with math.

____ + ____ = ____

You can use a ten-frame to show an addition fact with 5.

$5 + 3 = ?$

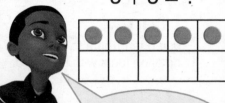

Start with 5. Then add 3 more.

5 and 3 more is 8.

There are 8 counters in the ten-frame.

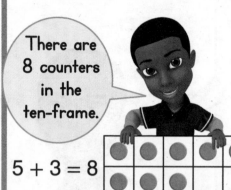

$5 + 3 = 8$

The ten-frame shows another addition fact. You have 8. Make 10.

2 boxes are empty. Add 2.

8 plus 2 more is 10.

$8 + 2 = 10$

Convince Me! How does a ten-frame help you add $5 + 4$?

☆ **Guided Practice** ☆

Look at the ten-frames.
Write an addition fact with 5.
Then write an addition fact for 10.

1.

$5 + \underline{2} = 7$

$7 + \underline{3} = 10$

2.
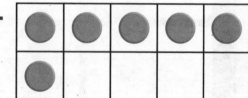

$5 + \underline{} = \underline{}$

$\underline{} + \underline{} = 10$

Tools Assessment

Look at the ten-frames.

Write an addition fact with 5.

Then write an addition fact for 10.

3.

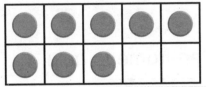

5 + _____ = _____

_____ + _____ = 10

4.

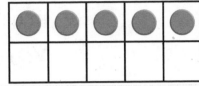

5 + _____ = _____

_____ + _____ = 10

5.

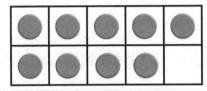

5 + _____ = _____

_____ + _____ = 10

6. Higher Order Thinking

Use 2 colors to draw counters in the ten-frames.

Match the addition equations.

Then write the missing numbers.

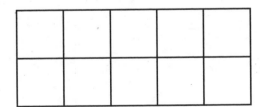

8 + _____ = 10

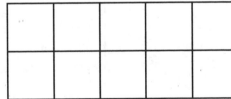

7 + _____ = 10

Which number will make 10?

7. Model

A team has 5 balls.

The coach brings 3 more balls.

How many balls does the team have now?

You can use the ten-frame to help.

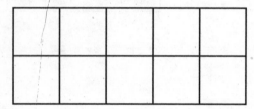

_____ balls

8. Model

Kami reads 5 books.

Sue reads 4 books.

How many books did the girls read in all?

You can use the ten-frame to help.

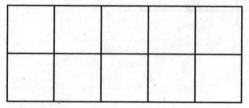

_____ books

9. Higher Order Thinking

Write a story with an addition fact for 10. Then write an equation for your story.

_____ + _____ = _____

10. ☑ Assessment Practice

Which sums equal 10?
Choose two that apply.

☐ 5 + 5 = _____

☐ 6 + 3 = _____

☐ 7 + 3 = _____

☐ 4 + 7 = _____

Name _____

Solve & Share

Write an addition equation for the green and yellow cubes in each cube tower. How are the addition equations the same? How are they different?

I can ...
use the same addends to write two different equations with the same sum.

I can also look for patterns.

_____ + _____ = _____

_____ + _____ = _____

You can change the order of the addends. The sum is the same.

4 and 2 is 6.

2 and 4 is 6.

$4 + 2 = 6$

$2 + 4 = 6$

You can write 2 addition equations.

4 plus 2 equals 6.

2 plus 4 equals 6.

$$\begin{array}{r} 4 \\ +\,2 \\ \hline 6 \end{array} \qquad \begin{array}{r} 2 \\ +\,4 \\ \hline 6 \end{array}$$

Convince Me! How can you use cubes to show that $5 + 3$ is the same as $3 + 5$?

☆ **Guided Practice** ☆ Color to change the order of the addends. Then write the addition equations.

1.

$3 + 4 = 7$

___ + ___ = ___

2.

___ + ___ = ___

___ + ___ = ___

Topic 2 | Lesson 5

Independent Practice Write the sum.
Then change the order of the addends.
Write the new addition equation.

3. 2 + 3 = ____

____ + ____ = ____

4. 1 + 6 = ____

____ + ____ = ____

5. ____ = 3 + 6

____ = ____ + ____

6. 5 + 2 = ____

____ + ____ = ____

7. 4 + 5 = ____

____ + ____ = ____

8. 6 + 2 = ____

____ + ____ = ____

 **Number Sense** Use the numbers on the cards to write two addition equations.

9.   **3** **8** **5**

____ + ____ = ____

____ + ____ = ____

10.   **4** **6** **2**

____ = ____ + ____

____ = ____ + ____

11. Model

Liza and Anna collect 6 cans.

They collect 4 more cans.

How many cans do they collect in all?

Draw a picture.

Then write two different addition equations.

_____ + _____ = _____

_____ + _____ = _____

12. Higher Order Thinking

Draw a picture of 5 birds.

Make some blue.

Make the rest red.

Write two addition equations
to tell about the picture.

_____ + _____ = _____

_____ + _____ = _____

13. ☑ **Assessment Practice**

Look at the two addition equations.

Which is the missing addend?

$9 = \underline{\ ?\ } + 2$

$9 = 2 + \underline{\ ?\ }$

Ⓐ 6

Ⓑ 7

Ⓒ 8

Ⓓ 9

Both equations
have a 2 and a 9.

Topic 2 | Lesson 5

Name _____

Solve & Share

There are 5 people on a bus.
It stops and 2 people get off.
Show how many people are still on the bus.
Then write the number.

_____ people are still on the bus.

You can use the number line to help you **count back** to subtract.

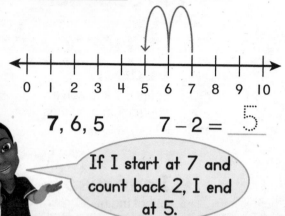

7, 6, 5 $7 - 2 = 5$

If I start at 7 and count back 2, I end at 5.

When you subtract 3, you can count back 3.

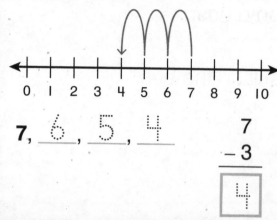

7, _6_ **,** _5_ **,** _4_

$\begin{array}{r} 7 \\ -3 \\ \hline \boxed{4} \end{array}$

When you subtract 0, you count back 0.

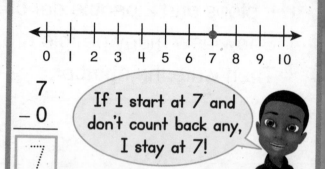

$\begin{array}{r} 7 \\ -0 \\ \hline \boxed{7} \end{array}$

If I start at 7 and don't count back any, I stay at 7!

Convince Me! Write subtraction equations to show counting back by 1, by 2, and by 3.

Count back to complete each subtraction fact.

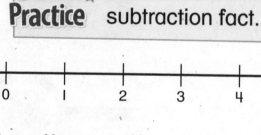

1. $\begin{array}{r} 4 \\ -1 \\ \hline \boxed{3} \end{array}$ $\begin{array}{r} 4 \\ -0 \\ \hline \boxed{4} \end{array}$

2. $\begin{array}{r} 6 \\ -0 \\ \hline \boxed{} \end{array}$ $\begin{array}{r} 6 \\ -2 \\ \hline \boxed{} \end{array}$

3. $\begin{array}{r} 9 \\ -5 \\ \hline \boxed{} \end{array}$ $\begin{array}{r} 9 \\ -3 \\ \hline \boxed{} \end{array}$

Topic 2 | Lesson 6

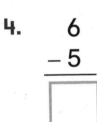 **Independent Practice**

Complete each subtraction fact.
Count back on the number line to help you.

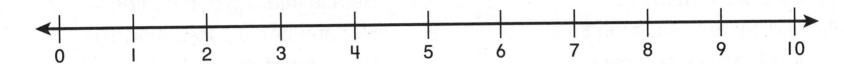

0 1 2 3 4 5 6 7 8 9 10

4.   6
    − 5
    ☐

5.   8
    − 0
    ☐

6.   10
    − 2
    ☐

7.   7
    − 4
    ☐

8.   9
    − 4
    ☐

Draw a picture.
Then write an equation and solve.

9. **Higher Order Thinking**

Amy and Ryan buy pencils.

Amy buys 10 pencils.

Ryan buys 8 pencils.

How many fewer pencils does Ryan buy?

_____ fewer pencils

10. Reasoning

Manny picks a number.

His number is 4 less than 8.

What is Manny's number?

_____ – _____ = _____

Manny's number is _____.

11. Reasoning

Beth is thinking of a number.

Her number is 0 less than 10.

What is Beth's number?

_____ – _____ = _____

Beth's number is _____.

12. Higher Order Thinking

Complete the subtraction equation.
Then write a story to match the equation.

$5 - 1 = $ _____

_____

_____

_____

13. ☑ **Assessment Practice**

Select the difference.

$10 - 3 = $ _____

Ⓐ 7

Ⓑ 5

Ⓒ 3

Ⓓ 1

You can draw
a number line
to help you
subtract.

Name _____

Solve & Share

Jenna has 6 balls.

Then 4 balls blow away.

How many balls does she have left?

Jenna says she can solve 6 − 4 by adding to 4.

What do you think Jenna did? Show your work.

I can ...
use addition facts I know to help me solve subtraction problems.

I can also look for patterns.

Addition fact: _____ + _____ = _____   So, _____ − _____ = _____.

You can use addition to help you subtract.

$7 - 3 = \boxed{?}$

$3 + \boxed{?} = 7$

What can I add to 3 to make 7? 3...4, 5, 6, 7.

$3 + \boxed{4} = 7$

The missing part is 4.

Think of the addition fact to solve the subtraction equation.

So, $7 - 3 = \boxed{4}$.

The difference is also 4.

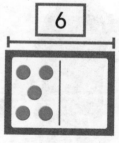

Convince Me! How can an addition fact help you solve $7 - 6$?

Guided Practice Think addition to help you subtract. Draw the missing part. Then write the missing numbers.

1.

5

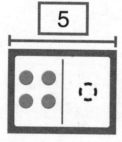

$5 - 4 = ?$

$4 + \underline{\quad} = 5$

So, $5 - 4 = \underline{\quad}$.

2.

6

$6 - 5 = ?$

$5 + \underline{\quad} = 6$

So, $6 - 5 = \underline{\quad}$.

Tools   Assessment

Think addition to help you subtract.
Draw the missing part.
Then write the missing numbers.

3.

8

6 + ____ = 8

So, 8 − 6 = ____ .

4.

7

4 + ____ = 7

So, 7 − 4 = ____ .

5.

4

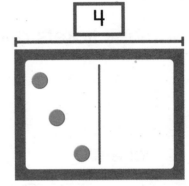

3 + ____ = 4

So, 4 − 3 = ____ .

6. Higher Order Thinking

Draw the shape to complete the equation.

You can use addition facts you know to help you subtract.

If ⬤ + △ = ◻ ,

then ◻ − ⬤ = ____ .

7. **Use Tools**

Pam needs 8 tickets for a ride.

She has 2 tickets.

How many tickets does Pam still need?

____ + ____ = ____

____ − ____ = ____

____ tickets

Which tool could help you solve this problem?

8. **Higher Order Thinking**

A box holds 6 crayons.

4 crayons are inside the box.

Kathy uses addition to find how many crayons are missing.

Is Kathy correct? Explain.

6 + 4 = 10
10 crayons are missing.

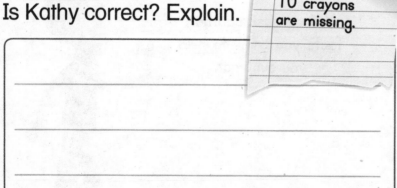

9. ☑ **Assessment Practice**

Which addition facts can help you solve 9 − 2?

Choose two that apply.

☐ 7 + 2 = 9

☐ 5 + 4 = 9

☐ 2 + 7 = 9

☐ 8 + 1 = 9

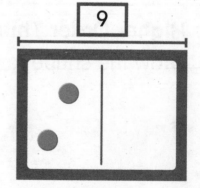

Activity

Solve & Share

6 fish swim by.
Some more fish join them.
Now there are 10 fish.
How many fish joined the group?

I can ...
draw pictures and write equations to help solve word problems.

I can also model with math.

Draw a picture.

Slater has 7 books.

He gives some books to Anna.
Now Slater has 2 books.
How many books did he give
Anna?

You can write an equation to model
the problem.

$$7 - \underline{\quad?\quad} = 2$$

Slater's books minus
the books he gives
Anna equals 2. So,
Slater gives Anna
5 books.

You can also count back from 7 to 2.

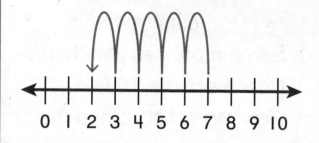

Count each jump from 7 to 2.
There are 5 jumps.
Slater gives Anna 5 books.

Convince Me!

7 cubes are on a table.
Some cubes fall off.
Now 3 cubes are on
the table.
How many cubes fell off
the table?

☆ **Guided** ☆
Practice

Draw a picture.
Then write an equation and solve.

1. Maria sees 3 blue birds.

She sees some red birds.
Maria sees 9 birds in all.
How many red birds
did Maria see?

____ red birds

Independent Practice ☆ Draw a picture. Then write an equation and solve.

2. Jamal picks 7 berries.
Then Ed picks more berries.
They pick 10 berries in all.
How many berries did Ed pick?

_____ berries

___ ◯ ___ = _____

3. Vicky has 8 flowers in her garden.
She picks some flowers.
Now there are 4 flowers left.
How many flowers did Vicky pick?

_____ flowers

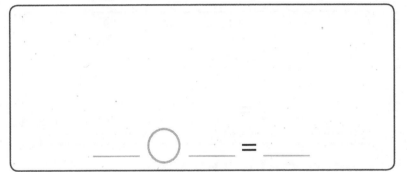

___ ◯ ___ = _____

4. Higher Order Thinking
Write a math story to match the picture.
Then write an equation.

_____
_____
_____
_____

___ = ___ ◯ ___

5. Make Sense

Charlie draws 9 stars.

Joey draws 4 stars.

How many fewer stars did Joey draw than Charlie?

_____ fewer stars

_____ = _____ ◯ _____

6. Make Sense

Brian finds 3 rocks on Monday.

He finds 7 rocks on Friday.

How many more rocks did Brian find on Friday than on Monday?

_____ more rocks

_____ = _____ ◯ _____

7. Higher Order Thinking

Write a math story and an equation to match the picture.

_____

_____

_____

_____

8. ☑ **Assessment Practice**

5 ducks are in a row.

More ducks join them.

Now there are 8 ducks.

How many ducks joined them?

Ⓐ 8 ducks

Ⓑ 5 ducks

Ⓒ 4 ducks

Ⓓ 3 ducks

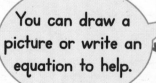

You can draw a picture or write an equation to help.

Name _____

Use counters and the part-part-whole mat to show different ways to make 10. Write the different ways in the table.

I can ...
look for patterns and use structure to solve problems.

I can also make 10 in different ways.

10

Thinking Habits

Is there a pattern?

How can I describe the pattern?

10 = [   ] + [   ]

10 = [   ] + [   ]

10 = [   ] + [   ]

10 = [   ] + [   ]

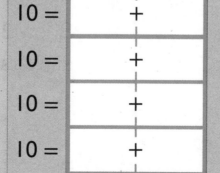

Some bears and lions want to cross the sea.

Only 10 animals can fit on a boat.

Show all the ways they can go on the boat.

How can I use structure to help me solve this problem?

Bears	Lions
0	10
1	9

I can use a table and patterns to help me find all the ways to make 10.

As the bears increase by 1...

Bears	Lions
0	10
1	9
2	8
3	7
4	6
5	5
6	4
7	3
8	2
9	1
10	0

...the lions decrease by 1...

The table helps me find all the ways the bears and lions can go.

Convince Me! Describe a pattern in the table that shows how many bears and lions there are.

☆ **Guided Practice** ☆ Use the table and patterns to help you solve the problem.

1. Patty has 4 dog stickers and 4 cat stickers.

She wants to put 6 stickers on a page of her book.

Show 3 ways Patty can put stickers on the page.

4	2

Topic 2 | Lesson 9

Tools   Assessment

Independent Practice ☆ Use patterns to help you solve each problem.

2. Max has 5 markers. He can put them in his desk or in his bag.

Complete the table to show all the ways.

Desk	Bag
0	____
____	4
2	3
3	____
____	1
____	____

3. Ms. Davis fills a box with 10 prizes. She has 7 balls and 7 balloons.

Complete the table to show all the ways.

7	3
6	4
5	____
4	____
____	____

Use patterns to help you solve the problem.

4. Higher Order Thinking

Julie plants 10 flowers.

She plants some by a tree and some in a box.

Find 3 ways Julie can plant the flowers.

____ by a tree and ____ in a box

____ by a tree and ____ in a box

____ by a tree and ____ in a box

Pieces of Fruit

Ed eats 7 pieces of fruit.

He eats strawberries and grapes.

Ben and Maria started tables to show all the ways Ed can eat the strawberries and grapes.

Ben

🍓	🍇
0	
1	
2	
3	
4	
5	
6	
7	

Maria

🍓	🍇
	6
	1
	4
	3
	2
	5
	0
	7

5. Model

Complete each table.

Use cubes or draw a picture to help you.

6. Look for Patterns

Describe one pattern in each table.

_____

_____

_____

Find a Match

Find a partner. Point to a clue. Read the clue.

Look below the clues to find a match. Write the clue letter in the box next to the match.

Find a match for every clue.

I can ...
add and subtract within 10.

I can also make math arguments.

Clues

A $3 + 1$

B $8 + 2$

C $4 + 3$

D $2 + 3$

E $1 + 2$

F $5 - 3$

G $9 - 1$

H $5 + 4$

| ☐ $3 + 2$ | ☐ $2 + 8$ | ☐ $2 + 1$ | ☐ $4 + 5$ |
| ☐ $3 + 4$ | ☐ $4 - 2$ | ☐ $1 + 3$ | ☐ $8 - 0$ |

Vocabulary Review

Word List
- doubles fact
- fewer
- more
- near doubles fact
- number line

Understand Vocabulary

1. Circle the addition equation that is shown on the number line.

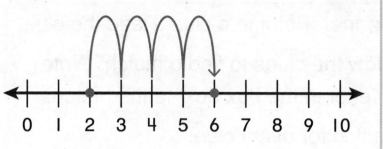

$1 + 1 = 2$ $2 + 1 = 3$ $2 + 4 = 6$ $3 + 3 = 6$

---

2. Cross out the problems that do **NOT** show doubles facts.

   $3 + 7$

   $2 + 2$

   $1 + 2$

3. Circle the near doubles facts.

   $4 + 5$

   $2 + 7$

   $3 + 6$

4. Circle the word that completes the sentence.
   Sam has 6 pens.
   Bev has 4 pens.
   Bev has 2 ____ pens than Sam.

   more   red   fewer

Use Vocabulary in Writing

5. Write and solve a story problem. Use at least one term from the Word List.

Name _____

Set A

8 peppers are in
the pot. You can
add 1 more by
counting 1 more.

Add 0, 1, or 2 to find the sum.
Write the addition fact.

1 more than 8 is 9.

$8 + 1 = 9$

1.

6

___ + ___ = ___

2.

9

___ + ___ = ___

Set B

You can use doubles facts to add.

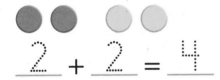

$2 + 2 = 4$

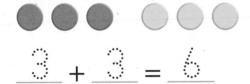

$3 + 3 = 6$

Both addends are the same.
They are doubles.

Write an addition equation for each doubles fact.

3.

___ + ___ = ___

4.

How many coins are there in all?

___ + ___ = ___

You can use doubles facts to add near doubles.

$2 + 2$ 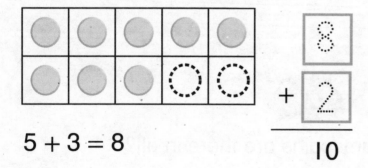 2 + 2 and 1 more

$2 + 2 = 4$ $2 + 3 = 5$

Find each sum.

5.

_____ + _____ = _____

_____ + _____ = _____

You can use a ten-frame to learn facts with 5.

Look at the addition equation. Draw counters in the frame.

8
+ 2
———
10

$5 + 3 = 8$

Draw counters and complete the addition problems.

6.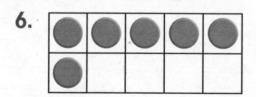

$5 + 1 =$ _____

+
———
10

Name _____

Set E

Find the sum.

$$2 + 5 = \underset{\text{sum}}{7}$$

You can change the order of the addends.

Write the new addition equation.

$$\underset{\text{sum}}{5} + 2 = 7$$

The sum is the same.

Write the sum. Then change the order of the addends and write a new addition equation.

7. $1 + 4 =$ ____

____ + ____ = ____

8. $6 + 3 =$ ____

____ + ____ = ____

When you change the order of the addends, the sum is the same.

Set F

You can subtract by counting back.

2 less than 9 is ___7___ .

Write the subtraction fact.

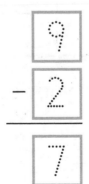

Count back to find the difference. Complete each subtraction fact.

9.

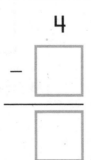

1 less than 4 is ____ .

10.

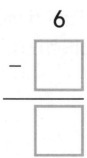

0 less than 6 is ____ .

You can think addition to help you subtract.

8

The missing part is 3.

$5 + \underline{3} = 8$

So, $8 - 5 = \underline{3}$.

Think addition to help you subtract.

11.

6

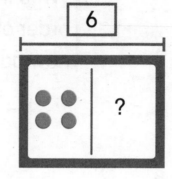

?

$4 + \underline{} = 6$

So, $6 - 4 = \underline{}$.

12.

7

?

$6 + \underline{} = 7$

So, $7 - 6 = \underline{}$.

Thinking Habits

Look For and Use Structure

Is there a pattern?

How can I describe the pattern?

Dani's family can care for 3 animals. Dani shows the ways they can care for cats and dogs.

13. Complete the table below.

Dogs	0	1	2	3
Cats				

14. Describe a pattern you see in the table.

_____

_____

98 ninety-eight

Topic 2 | Reteaching

1. Molly has 3 toy cars.
She gets 4 more as a gift.
How many toy cars does Molly have now?

Ⓐ 7

Ⓑ 8

Ⓒ 9

Ⓓ 10

2. Brad has 5 books.
His dad gives him 4 more.
How many books does Brad
have in all?

Ⓐ 1

Ⓑ 4

Ⓒ 5

Ⓓ 9

3. Sammy earns 7 stars in gym class.
He earns 3 stars in music class.
How many stars did Sammy earn in all?
Explain how you know.

_____ stars

4. Find 8 – 2.
Show your work.

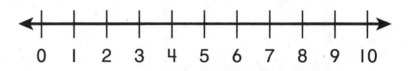

8 – 2 = _____

5. Write the doubles fact that will help you find $3 + 4$. Find the sum.

_____ + _____ = _____

$3 + 4 =$ _____

6. Yuri is thinking of a number.
His number is 0 less than 9.
Write an equation to find his number.

_____ − _____ = _____

7. A part is missing in the equations and model. Find the missing part.

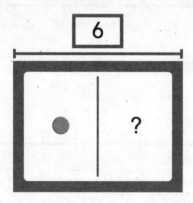

$1 +$ _____ $= 6$

$6 - 1 =$ _____

8. Choose two addition equations that match the picture.

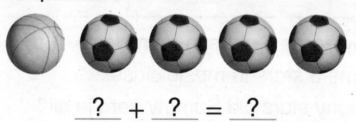

_____ $?$ + _____ $?$ = _____ $?$

☐ $1 + 4 = 5$

☐ $2 + 2 = 4$

☐ $3 + 1 = 4$

☐ $4 + 1 = 5$

☐ $3 + 3 = 6$

Topic 2 | Assessment Practice

Name _____

9. Choose two addition equations that can help find 9 − 3.

☐ 6 + 3 = 9

☐ 9 + 3 = 12

☐ 3 + 6 = 9

☐ 9 + 1 = 10

☐ 9 + 6 = 15

10. Find 5 + 4.

5 + 4 = _____

You can use a doubles fact to help.

11. Paul has 5 grapes.
His friend gives him 3 more.
How many grapes does Paul have now?

Ⓐ 8

Ⓑ 9

Ⓒ 10

Ⓓ 11

12. 3 frogs sit on a rock. 3 more join them.
How many frogs are there in all?
Draw a picture and write an equation.

_____ ◯ _____ = _____ frogs

13. Which is a doubles fact?

   Ⓐ   4 + 2 = 6

   Ⓑ   4 + 3 = 7

   Ⓒ   4 + 4 = 8

   Ⓓ   4 + 5 = 9

14. Erin is thinking of a number.
Her number is 5 less than 10.
What doubles fact could you use to find
Erin's number?

10 − 5 = ___?___

_____ + _____ = _____

15. Think addition to help you subtract.
Find the missing part.
Then write the numbers.

| 10 |

| 4 | ? |

4 + _____ = 10

10 − 4 = _____

16. Tina wants to buy 6 beads.
She can buy red or blue beads.
Complete the table to show all the ways Tina
can buy the beads.

Red	●	_____	_____	2	3	_____	5	_____
Blue	●	6	5	_____	_____	_____	_____	0

Name _____

Favorite Fruits

The first-grade students at Park School
took a vote on favorite fruits.
They made this chart.

Our Favorite Fruits	
Fruit	**Number of Votes**
Apple	5
Orange	4
Banana	6
Strawberry	2
Blueberry	3
Cherry	3
Peach	4
Grape	1

1. How many fewer students voted
for **Strawberry** than **Apple**?
Draw a picture and write an
equation to solve.

2. Laura says that she can use near doubles
to find the total number of votes for **Banana**
and **Strawberry**. Do you agree?

Circle **Yes** or **No**.

Show your work to explain.

3. 2 girls voted for **Orange**. Some boys voted for **Orange**.

How many boys voted for **Orange**?

Draw a picture to solve. Then write an addition or a subtraction equation.

Write how many boys voted for **Orange**.

_____

4. Fewer girls voted for **Banana** than boys. Complete the chart. Show the different ways boys and girls could have voted.

Girls	Boys

5. Gina says that **Orange** and **Blueberry** have the same total number of votes as **Cherry** and **Peach**. Is she correct? Explain how you know.

Topic 2 | Performance Task

Addition Facts to 20: Use Strategies

Essential Question: What strategies can you use for adding to 20?

Digital Resources

Interactive Student Edition   Activity   Visual Learning   Video   Practice

Assessment   Games   Tools   Glossary

Some animals have special teeth to eat plants.

Some animals have special teeth to eat meat.

Wow! Let's do this project and learn more.

ēnVision STEM Project: What Do They Eat?

Find Out Talk to friends and relatives about the things different animals eat. Ask how their teeth help them survive and meet their needs.

Journal: Make a Book Show what you found out. In your book, also:

- Draw pictures of animals and what they eat.
- Make up and solve addition problems about animals and what they eat.

Name _____

Review What You Know

⒜ Vocabulary

1. Circle the problem that shows a **double**.

   $5 + 5 = 10$

   $5 + 4 = 9$

   $5 + 3 = 8$

2. Circle the word that tells which strategy can be used to add the numbers.

   $7 + 8 = ?$

   doubles

   near doubles

   count back

3. Circle the **sum** in the problem below.

   $7 + 4 = 11$

Addition and Subtraction

4. Robin has 3 stamps. Joe gives her 4 stamps. How many stamps does Robin have now?

   _____ stamps

5. Jen has 8 cat treats. She feeds some treats to her cat. Jen has 4 treats left. How many treats did Jen feed her cat?

   _____ treats

Doubles Facts

6. Solve this doubles fact.

   $3 + 3 =$ _____

Name _____

PROJECT 3A

Can you see the gecko?

Project: Create an Animal Model

PROJECT 3B

Would you like to live on a boat?

Project: Make a Sailboat Model

PROJECT 3C

What is your favorite ride?

Project: Make a Poster about Roller Coasters

Video

Math Modeling

Go for a Spin

Before watching the video, think:

What was the last game you played? What kind of game was it? Video games, board games, and card games all have something in common. They need someone to test that the game is fun to play, and that it is fair.

I can ...

model with math to solve a problem that involves using different ways to make the same sum.

Solve & Share

Abby has 5 cubes.
Salina gives her 7 more cubes.
How many cubes does Abby have now?

Show your thinking.

I can ...
count on to add using a
number line.

I can also reason
about math.

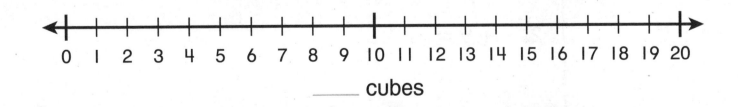

←|————|————|————|————|————|————|————|————|————|————|————|————|————|————|————|————|————|————|————|————|→
0 1 2 3 4 5 6 7 8 9 10 11 12 13 14 15 16 17 18 19 20

_____ cubes

Solve **7 + 8 = ?** using a number line.

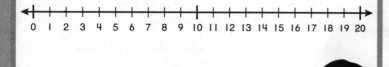

This number line has numbers from 0 to 20.

Find 7 on the number line. Then count on 8 more to add 7 + 8.

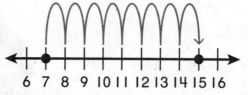

Start at 7 and make 8 jumps. You land on 15.

7 + 8 = 15.

If you start at 8 and make 7 jumps, you land on the same number.

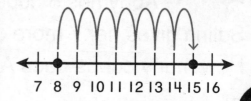

8 + 7 = 15 too!

Convince Me! How do you know where to start counting on?
How do you know how many to count on?

☆ **Guided Practice** ☆ Use the number line to count on. Write each sum.

1. 9 + 7 = ___16___

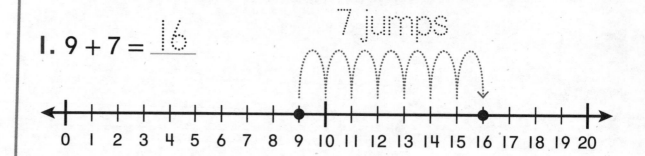

7 jumps

2. 9 + 9 = _____

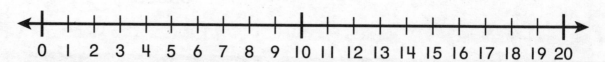

Topic 3 | Lesson 1

Independent Practice ☆   Use a number line. Count on to find each sum.

3. $7 + 4 =$ _____

4. $6 + 8 =$ _____

5. $9 + 4 =$ _____

6. $9 + 6 =$ _____

7. $7 + 7 =$ _____

8. $9 + 8 =$ _____

9. $6 + 4 =$ _____

10. $8 + 5 =$ _____

11. $3 + 9 =$ _____

Solve. Use a number line to count on.

12. **enVision**® STEM

Kim works at a zoo. She feeds the big cats 9 pounds of meat.
She feeds the tortoises 7 pounds of leaves and berries.

How many pounds of food does Kim feed the animals?

_____ pounds of food

13. Reasoning

Scott walks 6 blocks.

Then he walks 3 more blocks.

Write the numbers that will help find out how many blocks Scott walked in all.

Start at _____.   Count on _____ more.

$6 + 3 =$ _____

14. Reasoning

Ramona mails 3 letters.

Then she mails 8 more letters.

Write the numbers that will help find out how many letters Ramona mailed in all.

Start at _____.   Count on _____ more.

$3 + 8 =$ _____

15. Higher Order Thinking

Write and solve an addition story problem.

_____

_____

_____   _____ + _____ = _____

16. ☑ Assessment Practice

Solve $5 + 9 = ?$ on the number line. Show your work.

0 1 2 3 4 5 6 7 8 9 10 11 12 13 14 15 16 17 18 19 20

Lesson 3-2

Count On to Add Using an Open Number Line

Solve & Share

Arnie runs 6 miles on Thursday.
He runs 5 more miles on Friday.
How many miles did Arnie run in all?
Use the number line to show how you know.

I can ...
count on to add using an open number line.

I can also model with math.

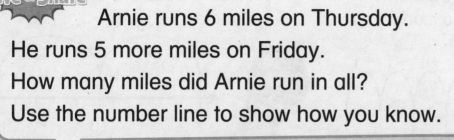

_____ miles

An **open number line** can help you add.

$$7 + 6 = ?$$

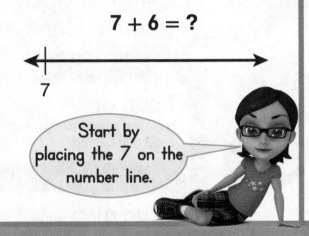

7

Start by placing the 7 on the number line.

Counting on by 1s is one way to add 6 more. Start at 7. Then count on 6 more.

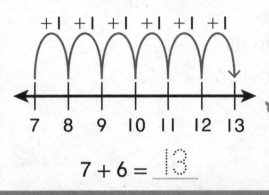

+1 +1 +1 +1 +1 +1

7 8 9 10 11 12 13

$$7 + 6 = \underline{13}$$

You can also break apart the 6. Adding 3 and 3 is one way to add 6 more.

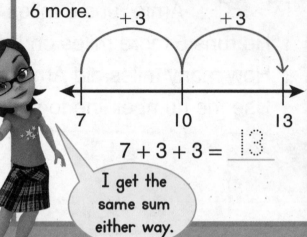

+3   +3

7   10   13

$$7 + 3 + 3 = \underline{13}$$

I get the same sum either way.

Convince Me! What number is always included on an open number line when you add?

☆ **Guided Practice** ☆ Use the open number line to solve. Show your work.

1. $7 + 5 = \underline{12}$

+3   +2

7   10   12

2. $6 + 2 = \underline{}$

Independent Practice ☆ Find each sum. Use the open number line to show your work.

3. $4 + 7 =$ _____

4. $8 + 8 =$ _____

5. $6 + 6 =$ _____

6. $9 + 7 =$ _____

7. (A-Z) **Vocabulary** Solve the problem.
Show your work on the **open number line** below.

$8 + 6 =$ _____

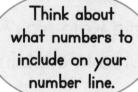

Think about what numbers to include on your number line.

8. Use Tools

Marco rides his bike 7 miles.

Then he rides 9 more miles.

How many miles did Marco ride in all?

_____ ◯ _____ = _____

_____ miles

9. Use Tools

Ana reads 10 books in January.

She reads 10 books in February.

How many books did Ana read in all?

_____ ◯ _____ = _____

_____ books

10. Higher Order Thinking

Kate has 8 roses.

She picks some more roses.

Now Kate has 17 roses.

How many roses did Kate pick?

Use words or pictures to explain

how you know.

11. ☑ Assessment Practice

Find the sum.

Show your work on the open number

line below.

$9 + 6 =$ _____

Name _____

Solve & Share

Carlos and Alisa each have the same number of books.

They each have more than 5 books.

How many books do they have in all?

Show your thinking below.

Let's look at some doubles facts that you may know.

$3 + 3 = 6$
$5 + 5 = 10$

Here are ways we can show these facts.

$3 + 3 = 6$ $5 + 5 = 10$

You can represent the doubles fact $6 + 6$ the same way.

$6 + 6 = 12$

This isn't a doubles fact.

$6 + 5 = 11$

Convince Me! Becca shows $6 + 7$ with cubes and says it is not a doubles fact. Is she correct? How do you know?

☆ **Guided Practice** ☆ Decide if the cubes show a doubles fact. Circle your answer. Then write an equation to match the cubes.

1.

Doubles Fact   **NOT** Doubles Fact

$\underline{5} + \underline{6} = \underline{11}$

2.

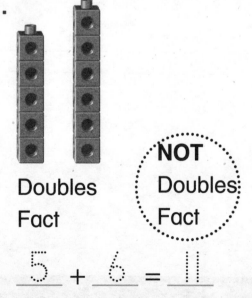

Doubles Fact   **NOT** Doubles Fact

$\underline{} + \underline{} = \underline{}$

Independent Practice Decide if each set of cubes shows a doubles fact.
Circle your answer. Write an equation to match the cubes.

3.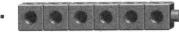

Doubles Fact   **NOT** Doubles Fact   ____ + ____ = ____

4.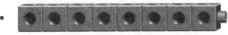

Doubles Fact   **NOT** Doubles Fact   ____ + ____ = ____

5.

Doubles Fact   **NOT** Doubles Fact

____ + ____ = ____

6.

Doubles Fact   **NOT** Doubles Fact

____ + ____ = ____

 Complete each doubles fact.

7. $0 + 0 =$ ☐ | 8. ☐ $= 9 + 9$ | 9. $8 + 8 =$ ☐ | 10. $5 + 5 =$ ☐

Draw cubes to help you solve each number story.
Then write an equation to match the problem.

11. Make Sense

Andrew and his sister each pick
10 flowers.
How many flowers did they pick in all?

____ ◯ ____ = ____

____ flowers

12. Make Sense

Pearl and Charlie each buy 5 books.
How many books did they buy in all?

____ ◯ ____ = ____

____ books

13. Higher Order Thinking

A hockey team plays 2 games.
The team scores the same number of
goals in each game.
The team scores 12 goals in all.
How many goals did the team score in
each game?

____ = ____ ◯ ____

____ goals in each game

14. ☑ **Assessment Practice** Which equations
show a doubles fact? Choose two that
apply.

☐ $7 + 7 = 14$

☐ $8 + 6 = 14$

☐ $8 + 8 = 16$

☐ $9 + 7 = 16$

Use cubes to
help if you
need to!

Name _____

Solve & Share

Carlos and I each pick 5 strawberries. What doubles fact shows how many strawberries we have in all?

If I pick 1 more strawberry, how could you find how many strawberries in all?

I can ...
use doubles facts to help solve doubles-plus facts.

I can also reason about math.

You can use doubles to find **doubles-plus facts**.

$$\begin{array}{r} 6 \\ +7 \\ \hline ? \end{array}$$

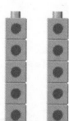

Doubles-plus facts are also called near doubles.

You already know 6 + 6.

$$\begin{array}{r} 6 \\ +6 \\ \hline 12 \end{array}$$

6 + 7 is 6 + 6 and 1 more.

$$\begin{array}{r} 6 \\ +6 \\ \hline 12 \end{array} \text{ and 1 more}$$

12 and 1 more is 13.

$$\begin{array}{r} 6 \\ +7 \\ \hline 13 \end{array}$$

Convince Me! How does knowing 7 + 7 help you find 7 + 8?

Guided Practice Add the doubles. Then use the doubles facts to help you solve the doubles-plus facts.

1.

$$\underline{5} + \underline{5} = \underline{10}$$

So, 5 + 7 = __12__.

2.

$$\underline{} + \underline{} = \underline{}$$

So, 8 + 9 = ___.

Topic 3 | Lesson 4

Name _____

Independent Practice — Add the doubles. Then use the doubles facts to help you solve the doubles-plus facts.

3.
```
   7        8
 + 7      + 7
 [   ]    [   ]
```

4.
```
   4        4
 + 4      + 6
 [   ]    [   ]
```

5.
```
   5        5
 + 5      + 6
 [   ]    [   ]
```

6.
```
   9        9
 + 9      + 10
 [   ]    [   ]
```

7.
```
   6        6
 + 6      + 7
 [   ]    [   ]
```

8.
```
   7        9
 + 7      + 7
 [   ]    [   ]
```

Use a doubles-plus fact to write an equation for the problem. Then draw a picture to match the equation.

9. Higher Order Thinking

Max has some blue marbles.

Tom has some red marbles.

Tom has 2 more marbles than Max.

How many marbles do they have in all?

___ ◯ ___ = ___

Solve each problem below.

Then write an equation to match the problem.

10. Reasoning

Carrie and Pete each pick 7 cherries.

Then Pete picks 1 more.

How many cherries do they have in all?

____ ◯ ____ = ____

____ cherries

11. Reasoning

Manny and Pam each buy 5 apples.

Then Pam buys 2 more.

How many apples do they have in all?

____ ◯ ____ = ____

____ apples

12. Higher Order Thinking

Laura has to solve $9 + 8$.

Explain how she could use $8 + 8$ to find the sum.

_____

_____

_____

_____

13. ☑ Assessment Practice

Use a doubles fact to help you find the missing addend.

$8 + \underline{\quad} = 17$

Ⓐ 8

Ⓑ 9

Ⓒ 7

Ⓓ 1

You can use doubles and a doubles-plus fact to help you solve the problem.

Name _____

Solve & Share

Andy says that he can find 9 + 5 by starting with 9 + 1 = 10.

What do you think about Andy's way?

Show your work and explain.

I can ...
make 10 to add numbers to 20.

I can also model with math.

Make 10 to help you add.

$$\begin{array}{r} 7 \\ +4 \\ \hline ? \end{array}$$

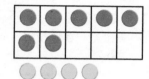

Move 3 counters from the 4 to join the 7.

Now I have 10 and 1.

$10 + 1$ is the same as $7 + 4$.

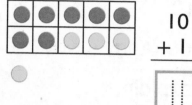

$$\begin{array}{r} 10 \\ +1 \\ \hline |1| \end{array}$$

$$\begin{array}{r} 10 \\ +1 \\ \hline |1| \end{array} \quad \text{so,} \quad \begin{array}{r} 7 \\ +4 \\ \hline |1| \end{array}$$

The sums are the same!

Convince Me! How would you make 10 to find the sum of $9 + 4$?

☆ **Guided Practice** ☆ Draw counters to make 10. Then write the sums.

1. $$\begin{array}{r} 7 \\ +6 \\ \hline ? \end{array}$$

$$\begin{array}{r} 10 \\ +3 \\ \hline |13| \end{array} \quad \text{so,} \quad \begin{array}{r} 7 \\ +6 \\ \hline \square \end{array}$$

2. $$\begin{array}{r} 8 \\ +6 \\ \hline ? \end{array}$$

$$\begin{array}{r} 10 \\ +4 \\ \hline \square \end{array} \quad \text{so,} \quad \begin{array}{r} 8 \\ +6 \\ \hline \square \end{array}$$

Topic 3 | Lesson 5

Tools Assessment

Independent Practice ☆ Draw counters to make 10. Then write the sums.

3. 7
   + 8
   ———
    ?

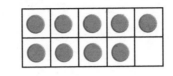

   10   7
  + 5   so, + 8
  ————   ————
  [ ]   [ ]

4. 9
   + 6
   ———
    ?

   10   9
  + 5   so, + 6
  ————   ————
  [ ]   [ ]

5. 7
   + 7
   ———
    ?

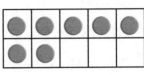

   10   7
  + 4   so, + 7
  ————   ————
  [ ]   [ ]

Draw counters to make 10. Use 2 different colors.
Then write the sums.

6. 6
   + 5
   ———
    ?

   10   6
  + 1   so, + 5
  ————   ————
  [ ]   [ ]

7. 4
   + 8
   ———
    ?

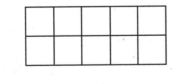

   10   4
  + 2   so, + 8
  ————   ————
  [ ]   [ ]

8. 9
   + 5
   ———
    ?

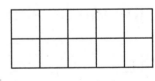

   10   9
  + 4   so, + 5
  ————   ————
  [ ]   [ ]

Draw counters to help you solve each problem below. Use 2 different colors.

9. Model

Carlos sees 7 yellow birds in a tree.
Then he sees 6 white birds.
How many birds does Carlos see in all?

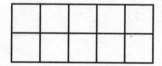

_____ birds

10. Model

Emily picks 8 red flowers.
Then she picks 8 yellow flowers.
How many flowers does Emily pick in all?

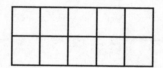

_____ flowers

11. Higher Order Thinking

Look at the model.
Complete the equations to match what the model shows.

$10 +$ _____ $=$ _____

So, _____ $+$ _____ $=$ _____ .

12. ☑ Assessment Practice

Which number belongs in the ?

$10 + 1 = 11$

So, $6 +$ ⬜ $= 11$

16   11   6   5
Ⓐ   Ⓑ   Ⓒ   Ⓓ

Name _____

Solve & Share

How can you make 10 to solve 8 + 5?
Show your work and explain.

I can ...
make 10 to add numbers to 20.

I can also make math arguments.

Make 10 to help you add. Find the sum.

$9 + 7 = ?$

9 is really close to 10. How can that help you find $9 + 7$?

You can use a number line to help you make 10.

You can think of $9 + 7$ as $9 + 1 + 6$, because $7 = 1 + 6$.

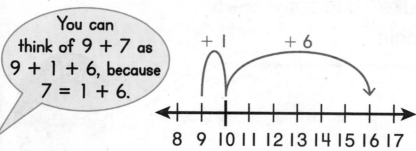

8 9 10 11 12 13 14 15 16 17

Think
9
$+ \boxed{1}$
―――
10

Think
10
$+ \boxed{6}$
―――
$\boxed{16}$

So, $9 + 7 = \underline{16}$.

Convince Me! How can you make 10 to find the sum of $7 + 6$?

☆ **Guided** ☆ Make 10 find the sum.
Practice Use the number line to help you.

1.

$\begin{array}{r} 8 \\ + 6 \\ \hline ? \end{array}$

Think
$\begin{array}{r} 8 \\ + \boxed{2} \\ \hline 10 \end{array}$

Think
$\begin{array}{r} 10 \\ + \boxed{4} \\ \hline \boxed{14} \end{array}$

So
$\begin{array}{r} 8 \\ + 6 \\ \hline \boxed{} \end{array}$

7 8 9 10 11 12 13 14 15 16 17 18 19 20

130 one hundred thirty

Tools   Assessment

☆   Make 10 to find each sum. Use a number line to help you.

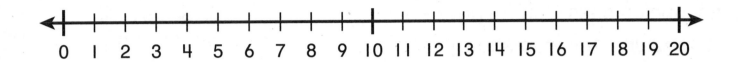

0 1 2 3 4 5 6 7 8 9 10 11 12 13 14 15 16 17 18 19 20

	Think	Think	So
2. 7	7	10	7
+ 8	+ ☐	+ ☐	+ 8
?	10	☐	☐

	Think	Think	So
3. 4	4	10	4
+ 9	+ ☐	+ ☐	+ 9
?	10	☐	☐

	Think	So
4. 8	10	8
+ 4	+ ☐	+ 4
?	☐	☐

	Think	So
5. 9	10	9
+ 7	+ ☐	+ 7
?	☐	☐

	Think	So
6. 6	10	6
+ 7	+ ☐	+ 7
?	☐	☐

7. **Number Sense** Jon adds 8 + 5.
First, he adds 8 + 2 to make 10.
What should he do next?

_____

_____

8. Look for Patterns

Conrad has 8 apples. Sam gives him 4 more.
How many apples does Conrad have now?
Use the open number line to show your work.

Can you break the problem into simpler parts?

Conrad has ＿＿ apples.

9. Higher Order Thinking

Pat makes 10 to solve $7 + 5$ by
changing the problem to $7 + 3 + 2$.
How does Pat make 10?

＿＿＿＿＿＿＿＿＿＿＿＿＿

＿＿＿＿＿＿＿＿＿＿＿＿＿

＿＿＿＿＿＿＿＿＿＿＿＿＿

＿＿＿＿＿＿＿＿＿＿＿＿＿

10. ☑ **Assessment Practice**

Which shows how to make 10
to add $9 + 6$?

Ⓐ $9 + 4 + 2$

Ⓑ $9 + 3 + 3$

Ⓒ $9 + 1 + 5$

Ⓓ $9 + 0 + 6$

Solve & Share

$8 + 6 = ?$

Choose a strategy to solve the problem.

Use words, objects, or pictures to explain your work.

I can ...
solve addition problems using different strategies.

I can also make math arguments.

Doubles   Near Doubles   Make 10

____ + ____ = ____

You can use different ways to remember addition facts.

Doubles   Near Doubles

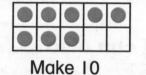

Make 10

4
+4

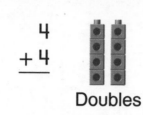

Doubles

Both addends are the same. These are doubles.

6 + 7

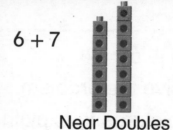

Near Doubles

The addends are 1 apart. These are near doubles.

8 + 5

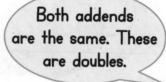

Make 10

10
+ 3

One addend is close to 10. You can make 10.

Convince Me! What strategy could you use to solve 7 + 8? Why is it a good strategy?

☆ **Guided Practice** ☆ Find each sum. Choose a strategy to use.

1.
```
   6
 + 6
```

12

2.
```
   9
 + 7
```
☐

3.
```
   6
 + 7
```
☐

4.
```
   8
 + 9
```
☐

Topic 3 | Lesson 7

Tools Assessment

Independent Practice ☆ Find each sum.

5.   6
   + 8
   ☐

6.   4
   + 9
   ☐

7.   7
   + 6
   ☐

8.   9
   + 8
   ☐

9.   8
   + 5
   ☐

10.   7
   + 4
   ☐

Find the missing number. Explain the strategy you used.

11. Algebra

Jan has 9 green marbles and some red marbles.
She has 11 marbles in all.

$9 + \underline{} = 11$

Jan has _____ red marbles.

_____

_____

_____

12. Make Sense

Brett has 8 shirts in his closet.

He puts more shirts in the dresser.

Brett has 16 shirts in all.

How many shirts did Brett put in the dresser?

_____ shirts in the dresser

13. Higher Order Thinking

Manuel and Jake have 13 pencils in all.

How many pencils could each boy have?

$13 =$ _____ $\bigcirc$ _____

Draw a picture to help you solve the problem.

14. ☑ **Assessment Practice** Which strategies could help you find $7 + 8$?
Choose three that apply.

Doubles ☐

Near Doubles ☐

Make 10 ☐

My Way ☐

Activity

Solve Addition Word Problems with Facts to 20

Solve & Share

Caleb has 4 more stickers than Zoe. Zoe has 5 stickers. How many stickers does Caleb have?

Use objects, drawings, or an equation to show your thinking.

I can ...
solve different types of addition word problems.

I can also make sense of problems.

Caleb has _____ stickers.

Visual Learning   A-Z Glossary

Tonya reads 5 books. She reads 7 fewer books than Seth.

How many books did Seth read?

This also means that Seth read 7 more books than Tonya.

What do you know?

Tonya read 5 books. Tonya read 7 fewer books than Seth.

What do you need to find out?

How many books Seth read

You can use counters.

You can write an equation.

$5 + 7 = 12$

Seth read 12 books!

Convince Me! Could you find out how many books Seth read by drawing a picture? Explain.

☆ **Guided Practice** ☆ Solve each problem. Use counters or draw a picture. Then write an equation.

1. Tim writes 9 stories. He writes 3 fewer stories than Daisy. How many stories did Daisy write?

2. Sherry reads 6 comic books. Dally reads 5 more comic books than Sherry. How many comic books did Dally read?

1. $9 \oplus 3 = \underline{\qquad}$

2. $\underline{\qquad} \bigcirc \underline{\qquad} = \underline{\qquad}$

Topic 3 | Lesson 8

Name _____

Independent Practice   Solve the problems with objects, drawings, or an equation. Show your work.

3. Tracy buys 10 buttons on Monday.
She buys more buttons on Tuesday.
Now she has 19 buttons.
How many buttons did Tracy buy on Tuesday?

_____ buttons

4. Jen has 9 coins.
Jen has 6 fewer coins than Owen.
How many coins does Owen have?

_____ coins

5. 14 cans are on the table.
5 cans are big and the rest are small.
How many small cans are on the table?

_____ small cans

6. Model

Leland cuts out 12 flowers.
How many can he color red
and how many can he color yellow?

Draw a picture and write an equation to help
solve the problem.

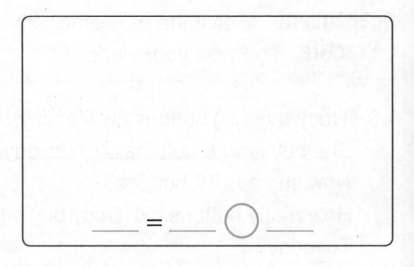

_____ = _____ ◯ _____

_____ red flowers   _____ yellow flowers

7. Higher Order Thinking

Nicole scored 8 goals this season.
She scored 9 fewer goals than Julien.
How many goals did Julien score?

Write this problem using the word *more*.

Nicole scored 8 goals this season.
Julien scored _____

_____

_____

8. ☑ Assessment Practice

Dan drinks 6 more glasses of water
than Becky.
Becky drinks 5 glasses of water.

How many glasses of water did Dan
drink?

Ⓐ $6 - 5 = 1$ glass of water

Ⓑ $6 + 5 = 11$ glasses of water

Ⓒ $11 + 6 = 17$ glasses of water

Ⓓ $11 - 6 = 5$ glasses of water

Name _____

Solve & Share

A pet store has 9 frogs.

5 of the frogs are green and the rest are brown.

Lidia adds 5 + 9 and says that the store has

14 brown frogs.

Circle if you **agree** or **do not agree** with Lidia.

Use pictures, words, or equations to explain.

I can ...
critique the thinking of others by using pictures, words, or equations.

I can also add and subtract correctly.

Agree   **Do Not Agree**

Thinking Habits

Can I improve on Lidia's thinking?

Are there mistakes in Lidia's thinking?

5 dogs are playing.
Some more dogs join.
Now 8 dogs are playing.

Mary says 13 dogs joined because $5 + 8 = 13$.

Joe says 3 dogs joined because $5 + 3 = 8$.

How can I decide if I agree with Mary or with Joe?

I can ask them questions, look for mistakes, or try to make their thinking clear to me.

I will draw a picture.

5 dogs   some more dogs

8 dogs

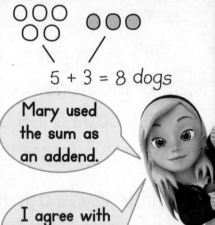

$5 + 3 = 8$ dogs

Mary used the sum as an addend.

I agree with Joe's thinking.

Convince Me! What question would you ask Joe to have him explain his thinking?

☆ **Guided Practice** ☆ Circle your answer. Use pictures, words, or equations to explain.

1. 9 cats chase a ball. Some cats stop to eat.
   Now 4 cats are chasing the ball.

   Stan says 13 cats stop to eat because $9 + 4 = 13$.
   Do you **agree** or **not agree** with Stan?

   Agree   **Not Agree**

Name _____

Independent Practice   Circle your answer.
Use pictures, words, or equations to explain.

2. 14 grapes sit in a bowl.   **Agree**   **Not Agree**
   9 are green. The rest are purple.
   How many are purple?

   Steve says 6 grapes are purple
   because $9 + 6 = 14$.
   Do you **agree** or **not agree** with Steve?

---

3. 11 oranges are in a bag.   **Agree**   **Not Agree**
   8 oranges fall out.
   How many oranges are left in the bag?

   Maria says 3 oranges are left
   because $11 - 8 = 3$.
   Do you **agree** or **not agree** with Maria?

Flower Vases Jill has 15 roses.
She wants to put some in a red vase
and some in a blue vase.

Help Jill solve the problem.
Answer the items below to check Jill's thinking.
Use pictures, words, or equations to explain.

4. Explain Jill says she can put an equal
number of roses in each vase.
She says she can write a doubles fact to
match the flowers in the blue and red vases.
Do you agree? Explain.

_____

_____

_____

_____

5. Model How could Jill use words or
drawings to show the problem?

_____

_____

_____

_____

Point & Tally

Find a partner. Get paper and a pencil.

Each partner chooses a different color: light blue or dark blue.

Partner 1 and Partner 2 each point to a black number at the same time. Both partners add those numbers.

If the answer is on your color, draw a tally mark.

Work until one partner draws twelve tally marks.

I can ...
add and subtract within 10.

I can also make math arguments.

Partner 1

2
0
3
1
4
2

| 3 | 7 | 4 | 10 | 9 | 2 |
| 5 | 1 | 0 | 8 | 3 | 6 |

Partner 2

4
6
5
0
1
2

| Tally Marks for Partner 1 | Tally Marks for Partner 2 |

Glossary

Understand Vocabulary

Word List
- doubles-plus fact
- make 10
- open number line
- whole

1. Circle **True** or **False**.

$10 + 5 = 15$ is a doubles-plus fact.

True   False

2. Circle **True** or **False**.

In the equation below, 8 is the whole.

$$10 + 8 = 18$$

True   False

---

3. Show how to make 10 to add $8 + 6$.

4. Write a doubles-plus fact.

5. Show 15 on the open number line.

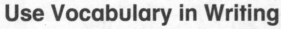

Use Vocabulary in Writing

6. What strategy could help you solve $7 + 8 = ?$
Use at least one term from the Word List.

Name _____

Set A _____

You can use a number line to add.
Start counting at one addend.
Count on the number of the other addend.

$$10 + 8 = \underline{\ ?\ }$$

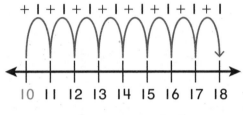

$$10 + 8 = \underline{18}$$

Reteaching

Use a number line.
Count on to find the sum.

1. $7 + 6 = \underline{\qquad}$

Set B _____

An open number line can help you add.
$$7 + 5 = \underline{\ ?\ }$$
Start with the first addend.

You can count on by 1s to add 5 more.

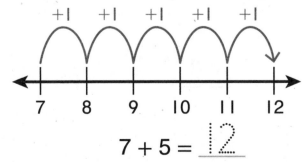

$$7 + 5 = \underline{12}$$

Use an open number line to solve
the problem. Show your work.

2. $4 + 9 = \underline{\qquad}$

A doubles-plus fact is a doubles fact and 1 or 2 more.

$$\begin{array}{r} 8 \\ +7 \\ \hline ? \end{array}$$

$$\begin{array}{r} 8 \\ +7 \\ \hline \boxed{15} \end{array}$$

$7 + 7 = 14.$

14 and 1 more is 15.

Add the doubles. Then use the doubles facts to help you solve the double-plus facts.

3.
$$\begin{array}{r} 5 \\ +5 \\ \hline \square \end{array}$$
$$\begin{array}{r} 6 \\ +5 \\ \hline \square \end{array}$$

4.
$$\begin{array}{r} 8 \\ +8 \\ \hline \square \end{array}$$
$$\begin{array}{r} 8 \\ +9 \\ \hline \square \end{array}$$

5.
$$\begin{array}{r} 6 \\ +6 \\ \hline \square \end{array}$$
$$\begin{array}{r} 8 \\ +6 \\ \hline \square \end{array}$$

6.
$$\begin{array}{r} 5 \\ +5 \\ \hline \square \end{array}$$
$$\begin{array}{r} 7 \\ +5 \\ \hline \square \end{array}$$

Set D

You can make 10 to add.

$$\begin{array}{r} 8 \\ +6 \\ \hline ? \end{array}$$

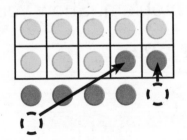

$$\begin{array}{r} 10 \\ +\ 4 \\ \hline \boxed{14} \end{array}$$
so,
$$\begin{array}{r} 8 \\ +6 \\ \hline \boxed{14} \end{array}$$

Make 10 to add. Draw counters in the ten-frame to help you.

7.
$$\begin{array}{r} 7 \\ +8 \\ \hline ? \end{array}$$

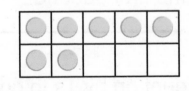

$$\begin{array}{r} 10 \\ +\ 5 \\ \hline \square \end{array}$$
so,
$$\begin{array}{r} 7 \\ +8 \\ \hline \square \end{array}$$

Name _____

Set E

You can choose different ways to add.

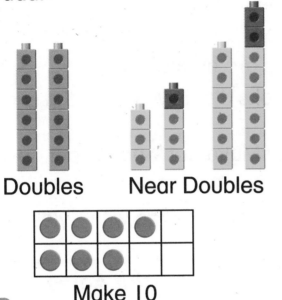

Doubles   Near Doubles

Make 10

Find each sum. Circle the strategy that you used.

8.   8
    + 4
    ☐

    Doubles   Make 10

    Near Doubles   My Way

9.   7
    + 8
    ☐

    Doubles   Make 10

    Near Doubles   My Way

Set F

You can write an equation to help you solve addition problems.
Sean plays in 8 soccer matches.
Karla plays in 3 more matches than Sean. In how many matches does Karla play?

8 ⊕ 3 = 11

Karla plays in 11 soccer matches.

Write an equation to solve the problem.

10. Leslie has 8 pencils.
    She has 9 fewer pencils than Grace.
    How many pencils does Grace have?

    ____ ◯ ____ = ____

    Grace has ____ pencils.

Thinking Habits

Critique Reasoning

What questions can I ask to understand other people's thinking?

Are there mistakes in other people's thinking?

Can I improve on other people's thinking?

Circle your answer.
Use pictures, words, or equations to explain.

11. 6 books are on a shelf.

Maya puts more books on the shelf.

Now 15 books are on the shelf.

How many books did Maya put on the shelf?

Kyle says that Maya put 9 books put on the shelf because $6 + 9 = 15$.

Do you **agree** or **not agree** with Kyle?

Agree   **Not Agree**

Name _____

1. Frank has 7 paper airplanes.
He makes 9 more.
How many paper airplanes does
Frank make in all?

Ⓐ 18

Ⓑ 17

Ⓒ 16

Ⓓ 15

2. Mark has 7 red marbles.
He has 8 blue marbles.
Which shows two ways to find
how many marbles Mark has
in all?

Ⓐ $7 + 8 = 14$ and $8 + 7 = 14$

Ⓑ $7 + 8 = 15$ and $8 + 7 = 15$

Ⓒ $7 + 7 = 14$ and $8 + 8 = 14$

Ⓓ $7 + 7 = 16$ and $8 + 8 = 16$

3. Use the open number line. Show how to count on to find $7 + 9$.
Then write the sum.

$7 + 9 =$ _____

4. Which are doubles facts?
Choose two that apply.

☐ $4 + 5 = 9$

☐ $10 + 5 = 15$

☐ $7 + 7 = 14$

☐ $10 + 10 = 20$

☐ $3 + 7 = 10$

5. 8 birds are in a tree.
9 more birds join them.
How many birds are in the tree now?
Write an equation to solve the problem.

_____ ◯ _____ = _____ birds

6. Gloria has 7 yellow pencils. She has 9 red pencils.
How many pencils does Gloria have in all? Explain.

Ⓐ 15 pencils; Doubling 7 gives 14, and 1 more is 15.

Ⓑ 19 pencils; Doubling 9 gives 18, and 1 more is 19.

Ⓒ 16 pencils; $7 + 3 = 10$, and 6 more is 16.

Ⓓ 17 pencils; $7 + 2 = 10$, and 7 more is 17.

Think about the strategies you have learned!

Topic 3 | Assessment Practice

7. Nina bakes 8 corn muffins on Tuesday.
She bakes 8 corn muffins on Wednesday.
How many corn muffins does Nina bake in all?

Which number line shows the problem?

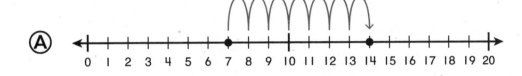

Ⓐ

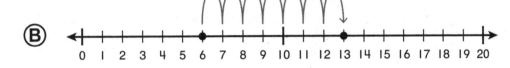

Ⓑ

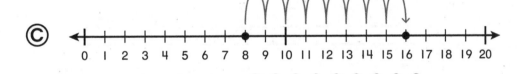

Ⓒ

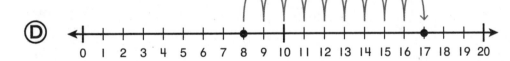

Ⓓ

8. Sandy makes 9 bracelets.
Then she makes 5 more bracelets.
How many bracelets does Sandy
have now?

Use words or pictures to explain.

9. Find 8 + 5. Make a 10 to add.

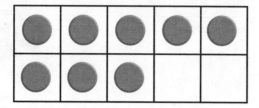

(A) 11

(B) 13

(C) 15

(D) 17

10. Maria has 8 more scarves than Lucy.
Lucy has 8 scarves.
How many scarves does Maria have?
Write an equation to solve.

_____ + _____ = _____

_____ scarves

11. There are 19 limes on the table.
10 fall to the floor.
Nicky says there are 9 limes left on the table.

Do you **agree** or **not agree** with Nicky's thinking?
Use pictures, words, or an equation to explain.

Agree   **Not Agree**

Topic 3 | Assessment Practice

Roger's Reading Record

Roger loves to read!

The chart shows how many books he read for six months.

Roger's Reading	
Month	Number of Books
January	9
February	7
March	6
April	8
May	5
June	8

1. How many books did Roger read in all in April and June? Write an equation to solve.

_____ + _____ = _____

_____ books

2. Roger read 4 more books in July than he did in January.

How many books did he read in July?
Draw a picture to solve.
Then write an equation to match.

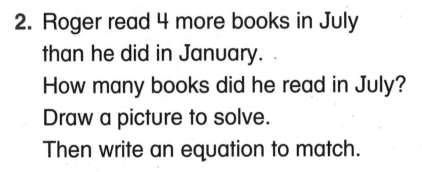

_____ + _____ = _____

He read _____ books in July.

3. In February, Tracy and Roger read 15 books in all. How many books did Tracy read in February?
Explain the strategy that you used to solve the problem.

_____

_____

_____

_____

_____ books

4. Sharon read 8 books in March. She said that she read 2 fewer books than Roger in March.

Do you **agree** or **not agree** with Sharon? Circle your answer.

Use pictures, words, or equations to explain.

Agree   **Not Agree**

TOPIC 4

Subtraction Facts to 20: Use Strategies

Essential Question: What strategies can you use while subtracting?

Digital Resources

Interactive Student Edition · Activity · Visual Learning · Video · Practice

Assessment · Games · Tools · Glossary

During the day, the sun appears to move across the sky.

At night, the sun is gone and the moon and stars appear.

Why do objects in the sky appear to move? Let's do this project and learn more.

enVision® STEM Project: Pattern of Day and Night

Find Out Talk to friends or relatives about how day and night changes on Earth.
How do day and night change as the Earth turns?

Journal: Make a Book Draw pictures of the day sky and the night sky. In your book, also:

• Draw objects that appear in the day and night skies.

• Write subtraction problems about objects that appear in the sky.

Name _____

Review What You Know

Vocabulary

1. Circle the number that is 4 **fewer** than 8.

   10

   6

   4

   0

2. Circle the **doubles fact**.

   $3 + 7 = 10$

   $8 + 0 = 8$

   $3 + 4 = 7$

   $6 + 6 = 12$

3. Circle the **doubles-plus fact**.

   $4 + 5 = 9$

   $3 + 6 = 9$

   $2 + 5 = 7$

   $4 + 4 = 8$

Subtraction Stories

4. Molly has 6 goldfish. She gives 3 goldfish to Nick.

   How many goldfish does Molly have now?

   Write an equation to show the difference.

   _____ – _____ = _____

5. Katie has 7 stamps. She gives 2 stamps to Jamie.

   How many stamps does Katie have now?

   Write an equation to show the difference.

   _____ – _____ = _____

Parts and Whole

6. Write the parts and the whole for $9 - 1 = 8$.

   Whole: _____

   Part: _____

   Part: _____

Name _____

PROJECT 4A

What pizza topping would make you laugh?

Project: Write a Funny Pizza Poem

PROJECT 4B

Do you know your vegetables?

Project: Play Vegetable Subtraction

PROJECT 4C

How can you play baseball without a ball?

Project: Play Baseball!

PROJECT 4D

How much do some classroom items cost?

Project: Buy Classroom Items

Solve & Share

Marc has 13 erasers.
He gives 5 of them to Troy.
How many erasers does Marc have now?

Show your thinking in the space below.

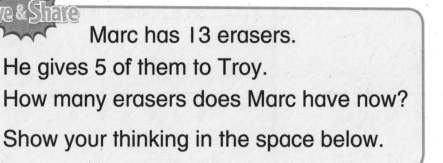

I can ...
subtract using a number line.

I can also reason about math.

Marc has _____ erasers now.

You can count back or count on to subtract.

Let's try with 11 − 5.

You can count back on a number line to subtract 11 − 5.

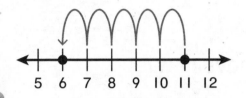

Start at 11.
Count back 5.
11 − 5 = 6

You can also count on to subtract 11 − 5 on a number line.

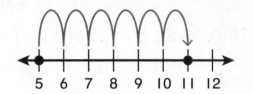

Start at 5.
Count on 6 to get to 11.
5 + 6 = 11,
so 11 − 5 = 6.

Convince Me! How can you use a number line to solve 9 − 5?

☆ **Guided Practice** ☆ Find the difference. Use the number line.

1. 11 − 3 = ___8___

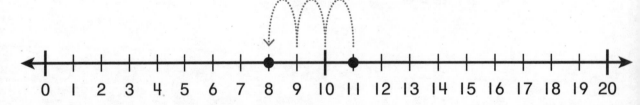

2. ___ = 15 − 6

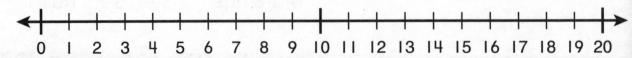

Topic 4 | Lesson 1

Tools   Assessment

Independent Practice   Find the difference.
Use the number line.

3. $11 - 6 =$ _____

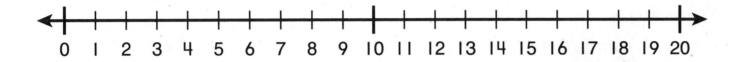

0 1 2 3 4 5 6 7 8 9 10 11 12 13 14 15 16 17 18 19 20

4. _____ $= 7 - 7$

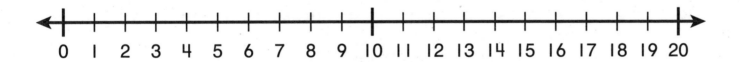

0 1 2 3 4 5 6 7 8 9 10 11 12 13 14 15 16 17 18 19 20

5. $15 -$ _____ $= 7$

0 1 2 3 4 5 6 7 8 9 10 11 12 13 14 15 16 17 18 19 20

You can draw a number line.

6. Use Tools

Help David find 16 – 7 on a number line.
Fill in the blanks.

Start at _____. Count back _____. 16 – 7 = _____

7. Higher Order Thinking

Jenny draws 14 frogs. Adam draws 6 frogs.
How many more frogs does Jenny draw than Adam?
Write an equation.

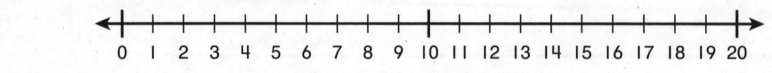

_____ ◯ _____ = _____   _____ more frogs

8. ☑ Assessment Practice

Use the number line to find 15 – 9.
Show your work.

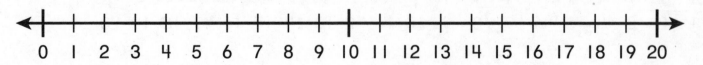

15 – 9 = _____

Activity

Solve & Share

How can thinking about 10 help you find 11 − 7?

I can ...
make subtraction easier by making 10 to subtract.

I can also use math tools correctly.

_____ − _____ = _____

Visual Learning  A-Z Glossary

You can make 10 to help you subtract.

$$12 - 5 = ?$$

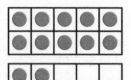

Start with 12.

Subtract 2 to get to 10.

I subtract the extra ones to get to 10.

Subtract 3 more because $5 = 2 + 3$.

I subtracted 5 in all.

There are 7 left.

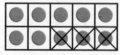

$12 - 5 = 7$
The answer is 7!

Convince Me! How can finding $14 - 4$ help you find $14 - 6$?

☆ **Guided Practice** ☆ Make 10 to subtract.
Complete each subtraction fact.

1. $16 - 7 = ?$

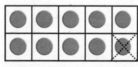
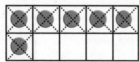

$16 - \underline{6} = 10$

$10 - \underline{1} = \underline{9}$

So, $16 - 7 = \underline{9}$.

2. $13 - 8 = ?$

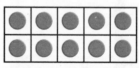
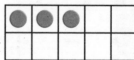

$13 - \underline{} = 10$

$10 - \underline{} = \underline{}$

So, $13 - 8 = \underline{}$.

166 one hundred sixty-six

Topic 4 | Lesson 2

Independent Practice

Make 10 to subtract.
Complete each subtraction fact.

3.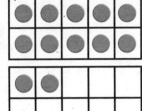

12 − 4 = _____

4.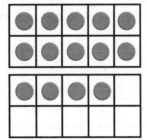

14 − 6 = _____

5.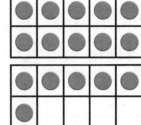

16 − 9 = _____

6.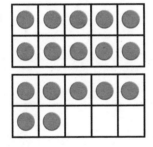

17 − 8 = _____

7.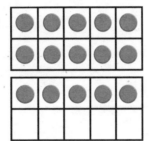

15 − 7 = _____

8.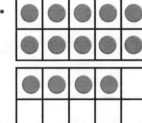

14 − 9 = _____

 Show your work.
Draw counters in the ten-frames.

9. Number Sense

Show how you can make 10 to find 13 − 6.

13 − 6 = _____

10. Use Tools

Kyle bakes 12 muffins.

His friends eat 6 muffins.

How many muffins are left?

Make 10 to subtract.

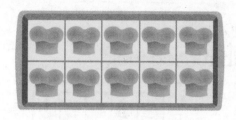

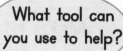

What tool can you use to help?

$12 - \underline{} = 10$

$10 - \underline{} = \underline{}$ muffins

---

11. Higher Order Thinking

Zak makes 10 to solve $12 - 5$.

He changes the problem to $12 - 2 - 3$.

How does Zak make 10?

_____

_____

_____

---

12. ☑ **Assessment Practice** Draw lines.

Match each pair of ten-frames with the equations
that show how to subtract by making 10.

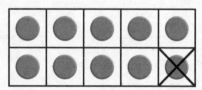 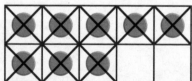

$18 - 8 = 10, 10 - 1 = 9$

$18 - 8 = 10, 10 - 2 = 8$

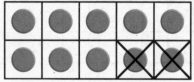 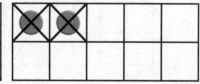

$12 - 2 = 10, 10 - 2 = 8$

$12 - 3 = 9, 9 - 1 = 8$

Name _____

Solve & Share

Emily counts on to find 13 – 6.

She makes 10 while counting.

Use the ten-frames to explain what Emily could have done.

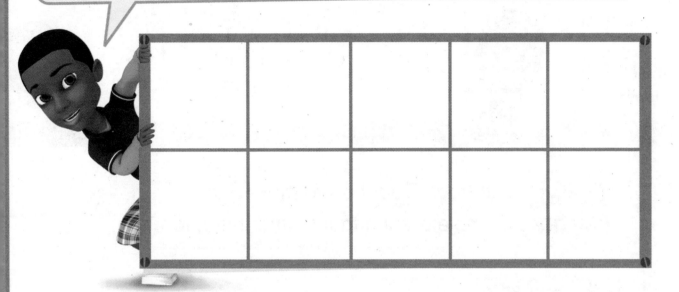

13 – 6 = ____

Counting on to make 10 can help you subtract.

$14 - 6 = \underline{\ ?\ }$

Start with 6.

Add 4 to make 10.

$6 + \underline{4} = 10$

I add 4 to 6 to make 10.

Add 4 more to make 14.

$10 + \underline{4} = 14$

How many did you count on?

$6 + \underline{4} + \underline{4} = 14$

$6 + \underline{8} = 14$

I added 8 to 6 to make 14. So, $14 - 6 = 8$.

Convince Me! How can counting on to make 10 help you find $15 - 8$?

☆ **Guided Practice** ☆ Subtract. Count on to make 10.
Complete each fact to find the difference.

1. $13 - 9 = ?$

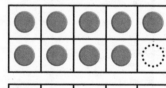

$9 + \underline{1} = 10$

$10 + \underline{3} = 13$

$9 + \underline{\ \ } = 13$, so $13 - 9 = \underline{\ \ }$.

Independent Practice

Subtract. Count on to make 10.
Show your work, and complete the facts.

2. $12 - 8 = ?$

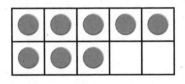

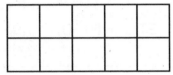

$8 + \underline{\quad} = 10$

$10 + \underline{\quad} = 12$

$8 + \underline{\quad} = 12$, so $12 - 8 = \underline{\quad}$.

3. $15 - 7 = ?$

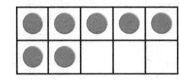

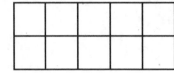

$7 + \underline{\quad} = 10$

$10 + \underline{\quad} = 15$

$7 + \underline{\quad} = 15$, so $15 - 7 = \underline{\quad}$.

4. $14 - 5 = \underline{\quad}$

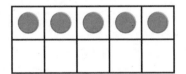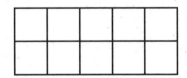

5. $16 - 9 = \underline{\quad}$

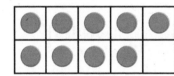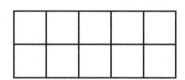

6. enVision® STEM

Hoshi watches 13 sunrises or sunsets.
She watches 5 sunsets.
How many sunrises did Hoshi watch?
Make 10 to help you solve.

$5 + \underline{\quad} = 10$

$10 + \underline{\quad} = 13$

$5 + \underline{\quad} = 13$, so $13 - 5 = \underline{\quad}$ sunrises.

7. Make Sense

Sage has 13 stickers.

She gives 7 to her brother.

How many stickers does Sage have left?

How can you make 10 to solve?

Sage has _____ stickers left.

8. Higher Order Thinking

Colin has 12 toys.

He gives 9 toys away.

How many toys does Colin have left?

Make 10 to solve. Show your work.

_____ ◯ _____ = _____

Colin has _____ toys left.

9. ☑ Assessment Practice

Which equations show how to make 10 to solve $16 - 7 = ?$

Ⓐ $16 - 10 = 6$

Ⓑ $7 + 3 = 10, 10 + 6 = 16, 3 + 6 = 9$

Ⓒ $7 + 3 = 10, 10 + 7 = 17, 3 + 7 = 10$

Ⓓ $10 + 7 = 17$

Name _____

Solve & Share

Write 2 addition and 2 subtraction facts.
Use the numbers 8, 9, and 17.
Use cubes to help you.

I can ...
make addition and subtraction facts using the same three numbers.

I can also look for patterns.

___ + ___ = ___   ___ - ___ = ___

___ + ___ = ___   ___ - ___ = ___

Write 2 addition facts for this model.

$$9 + 6 = 15$$

15

Add the parts in any order.

$$6 + 9 = 15$$

You can also write 2 subtraction facts.

15

Subtract 1 part from the whole.

$$15 - 6 = 9$$

Subtract the other part from the whole.

15

$$15 - 9 = 6$$

These are **related facts**.

$$9 + 6 = 15$$
$$6 + 9 = 15$$
$$15 - 6 = 9$$
$$15 - 9 = 6$$

They are a **fact family**.

Convince Me! How are $15 - 6 = 9$ and $15 - 9 = 6$ related?

☆ **Guided Practice** Write the fact family for each model.

1.

14

$$14 = 6 + 8$$
$$14 = 8 + 6$$
$$8 = 14 - 6$$
$$6 = 14 - 8$$

2.

16

$$\underline{} + \underline{} = \underline{}$$
$$\underline{} + \underline{} = \underline{}$$
$$\underline{} - \underline{} = \underline{}$$
$$\underline{} - \underline{} = \underline{}$$

Independent Practice Write the fact family for each model.

3.

17

9 | 8

___ + ___ = ___

___ + ___ = ___

___ − ___ = ___

___ − ___ = ___

4.

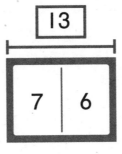

13

7 | 6

___ = ___ + ___

___ = ___ + ___

___ = ___ − ___

___ = ___ − ___

5.

12

4 | 8

___ + ___ = ___

___ + ___ = ___

___ − ___ = ___

___ − ___ = ___

---

6. Number Sense

Are the following equations a fact family?

Explain your answer.

What is the whole?
What are the parts?

$9 + 5 = 14$

$15 − 5 = 10$

$4 + 4 = 8$

$15 = 6 + 9$

_____

_____

_____

_____

7. Look for Patterns

Pat arranged the counters below.
Write the fact family for the set of counters.

___ = ___ + ___

___ = ___ + ___

___ = ___ − ___

___ = ___ − ___

8. Higher Order Thinking

Tanya has 8 stickers.

Miguel gives her 5 more.

How many stickers does Tanya have in all?

Write an equation to solve the problem.
Then complete the fact family.

___ ◯ ___ = ___ stickers

___ ◯ ___ = ___

___ ◯ ___ = ___

___ ◯ ___ = ___

9. ☑ **Assessment Practice**

Write a fact family to match the picture
of the yellow robots and green robots.

___ + ___ = ___

___ + ___ = ___

___ − ___ = ___

___ − ___ = ___

Name _____

Solve & Share

$12 - 9 = ?$

How can a related fact help you find $12 - 9$?
Write the related addition and subtraction facts.
You can use counters to help.

I can ...
use addition facts to find subtraction facts.

I can also look for things that repeat.

_____ + _____ = _____   _____ − _____ = _____

13 − 8 = ?

Use addition to help you subtract.

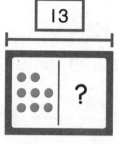

What can I add to 8 to make 13?

13

 ?

8 + ? = 13

Model the addition fact.

13

I can add 2 to get to 10 and then 3 more to get to 13. That's 5!

Convince Me! How could you use addition to solve 16 − 9?

☆ **Guided Practice** ☆ Complete each model. Then complete the equations.

1. 14 − 8 = ?

14

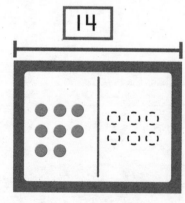

8 + _6_ = 14

14 − 8 = _6_

2. 17 − 9 = ?

17

9 + ___ = 17

17 − 9 = ___

Independent Practice Complete each model.
Then complete the equations.

3. 13 − 9 = ?

9 + ____ = 13

13 − 9 = ____

4. 20 − 10 = ?

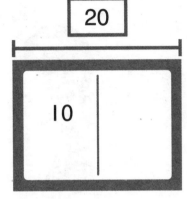

10 + ____ = 20

20 − 10 = ____

5. 15 − 7 = ?

7 + ____ = 15

15 − 7 = ____

Draw the missing shape for each problem.

6. Algebra

If ● + ■ = ▲ ,

then ▲ − ■ = ____ .

7. Algebra

If ▬ − ▮ = ▮ ,

then ____ + ▮ = ▬ .

Problem Solving

Solve each problem.

Write a related addition fact and subtraction fact to help you.

8. Generalize

There are 17 robot parts.

Fred uses some of the parts.

Now there are 8 left.

How many parts did Fred use?

_____ + _____ = _____

_____ − _____ = _____ _____ parts

9. Generalize

Maria invites 10 friends to her party.

3 cannot come.

How many friends will be at Maria's party?

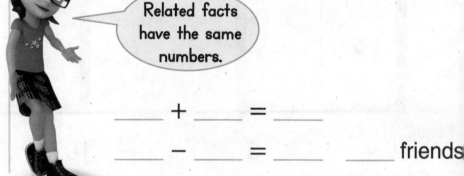

Related facts have the same numbers.

_____ + _____ = _____

_____ − _____ = _____ _____ friends

10. Higher Order Thinking

Write a subtraction equation with 11. Then write a related addition fact you could use to solve it.

_____ ◯ _____ = _____

_____ ◯ _____ = _____

11. ☑ Assessment Practice

Write an addition fact that will help you solve 13 − 7 = ?.

_____ + _____ = _____

Activity

Lesson 4-6

Continue to Use Addition to Subtract

I can ...
use addition facts to find subtraction facts.

I can also reason about math.

Solve & Share

Complete the subtraction facts.

Draw lines from the subtraction facts to the addition facts that can help you.

How are the subtraction facts and the addition facts alike?

$16 - 9 =$ _____

$17 - 8 =$ _____

$18 - 9 =$ _____

$16 - 7 =$ _____

$17 - 9 =$ _____

$9 + 9 = 18$

$7 + 6 = 13$

$9 + 8 = 17$

$6 + 6 = 12$

$9 + 7 = 16$

Every subtraction fact has a related addition fact.

$$15 - 7 = \boxed{?}$$

You can think addition to help you subtract.

$$15 - 7 = \boxed{?}$$

$$7 + \boxed{?} = 15$$

 I add 8 to 7 to make 15.

$$7 + \boxed{8} = 15$$

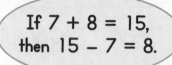 If 7 + 8 = 15, then 15 − 7 = 8.

$$15 - 7 = \boxed{8}$$

Convince Me! How does the fact 6 + 9 = 15 help you solve 15 − 6?

☆ **Guided Practice** ☆ Complete the addition fact. Then solve the related subtraction fact.

1.
$$9 + \boxed{5} = 14$$
$$14 - 9 = \boxed{5}$$

2.
$$10 + \boxed{\ } = 20$$
$$20 - 10 = \boxed{\ }$$

3.
$$7 + \boxed{\ } = 11$$
$$11 - 7 = \boxed{\ }$$

4.
$$8 + \boxed{\ } = 13$$
$$13 - 8 = \boxed{\ }$$

Topic 4 | Lesson 6

Independent Practice ✫ Think addition to solve each subtraction fact.

5. 15
    − 8
    ⬜

6. 18
    − 9
    ⬜

7. 13
    − 9
    ⬜

8. 11
    − 2
    ⬜

9. 16
    − 7
    ⬜

10. 14
     − 8
     ⬜

11. 17
     − 7
     ⬜

12. 12
     − 4
     ⬜

A-Z Vocabulary Circle **Yes** or **No** to show whether or not the **related facts** are correct.

13. If 8 + 8 = 16,

then 16 − 8 = 8.

Yes   No

14. If 7 + 6 = 13,

then 16 − 7 = 3.

Yes   No

15. **Reasoning**

Sam has some crayons.

He finds 6 more.

Now Sam has 13 crayons.

How many crayons did Sam have
before he found more?

_____ + _____ = _____

_____ − _____ = _____

_____ crayons

How are the
numbers
in the problem
related?

16. **Higher Order Thinking**

Solve 13 − 4.

Use pictures, numbers, or words to show
how you solved it.

17. ☑ **Assessment Practice**

Which related addition fact helps you
solve 14 − 6 = ?

Ⓐ 8 + 8 = 16

Ⓑ 6 + 8 = 14

Ⓒ 7 + 7 = 14

Ⓓ 6 + 9 = 15

Name _____

Solve & Share

Choose a strategy to solve the problem.

Jeff has 12 apples. He gives away 6 apples.
How many apples are left?
Use words, objects, or pictures to explain your work.

I can ...
explain the strategies I use to solve subtraction problems.

I can also make math arguments.

_____ − _____ = _____

You can use different ways to solve subtraction facts.

$10 - 3 = ?$

You can count on or back to solve subtraction facts.

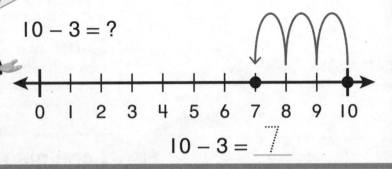

0 1 2 3 4 5 6 7 8 9 10

$10 - 3 = \underline{7}$

You can make a 10 to subtract $12 - 8$.

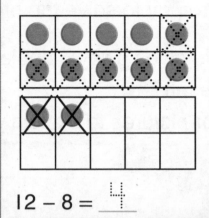

$12 - 8 = \underline{4}$

You can think addition to subtract $14 - 6$.

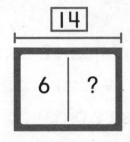

14

6 | ?

$6 + \underline{8} = 14$

$14 - 6 = \underline{8}$

Convince Me! Use the number line above. How can you count on to find $10 - 3$?

☆ **Guided Practice** ☆ Find each difference. Be ready to tell how you solved.

1. $\begin{array}{r} 15 \\ -9 \\ \hline \boxed{6} \end{array}$

2. $\begin{array}{r} 9 \\ -7 \\ \hline \boxed{} \end{array}$

3. $\begin{array}{r} 13 \\ -3 \\ \hline \boxed{} \end{array}$

4. $\begin{array}{r} 17 \\ -8 \\ \hline \boxed{} \end{array}$

Tools Assessment

Independent Practice ✩ Choose a strategy to find each difference.

5.
```
   15
 –  5
 ┌──┐
 └──┘
```

6.
```
    9
 –  3
 ┌──┐
 └──┘
```

7.
```
   14
 –  9
 ┌──┐
 └──┘
```

8.
```
   12
 –  4
 ┌──┐
 └──┘
```

9.
```
    7
 –  7
 ┌──┐
 └──┘
```

10.
```
   13
 –  5
 ┌──┐
 └──┘
```

Write a subtraction equation to solve the problem.
Explain which strategy you used.

11. **Higher Order Thinking**

Maya has a box of 16 crayons.

7 crayons are broken.

How many crayons are **NOT** broken?

_____ – _____ = _____

_____ crayons

12. Make Sense

Holly has 11 books.

She has 4 more books than Jack.

How many books does Jack have?

Jack has _____ books.

What's your plan for solving the problem? What else can you try if you get stuck?

13. Higher Order Thinking

What strategy would you use to solve $10 - 6$?

_____

_____

_____

14. ☑ Assessment Practice

Which addition facts will help you solve $16 - 9 = ?$

Choose two.

☐ $9 + 7 = 16$

☐ $7 + 10 = 17$

☐ $7 + 9 = 16$

☐ $10 + 7 = 17$

Name _____

Some books are on a shelf.
Aiden puts 4 more books on the shelf.
Now there are 12 books.
How many books were on the shelf to start?

I can ...
solve different kinds of
addition and subtraction
problems.

I can also reason
about math.

Use objects,
drawings, or
equations to show
your thinking.

There were _____ books to start.

Hunter has some pencils.

He gives 6 of them to Margo.

Now Hunter has 5 pencils.

How many pencils did Hunter start with?

Write an equation to show the problem.

Hunter gives 6 pencils away. He has 5 left.

$$\underline{\quad?\quad} - 6 = 5$$

You know two parts. Add to find the whole.

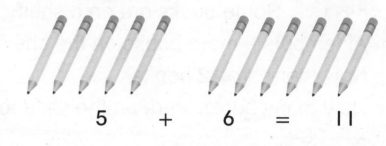

$$5 \quad + \quad 6 \quad = \quad 11$$

So, $\underline{11} - 6 = 5$.

Hunter starts with 11 pencils.

Convince Me! Sue has 8 crayons. She gets 8 more. How many crayons does she have now? Would you add or subtract to solve the problem? Explain.

☆ **Guided Practice** ☆ Write an equation to match the story and solve. Draw a picture to help.

1. Cal rides his bike on Monday.

   He rides 8 miles on Tuesday. He rides 14 miles in all.

   How many miles did Cal ride on Monday?

$$\underline{\qquad} \; \bigoplus \; \underline{8} \; = \; \underline{14}$$

miles on Monday   miles on Tuesday   miles in all

Name _____

Independent Practice

Write an equation to match the story. Then solve. Draw a picture to help.

2. Maggie wrote 9 pages of a story yesterday.
She writes some more pages today.
She writes 15 pages in all.
How many pages did Maggie write today?

___ ◯ ___ = ___

___ pages

3. Gemma has 6 games.
Chris has 13 games. How many fewer games does Gemma have than Chris?

___ ◯ ___ = ___

___ fewer games

4. Lily has 7 fewer ribbons than Dora.
Lily has 13 ribbons.
How many ribbons does Dora have?

___ ◯ ___ = ___

___ ribbons

5. Reasoning

Will has 11 toy cars.

How many can he put in his red case?

How many can he put in his blue case?

Draw a picture and write an equation to solve.

11 = ____ ◯ ____

6. Higher Order Thinking

Write an addition and subtraction equation to match the problem. Then solve.

Jon has 9 oranges.

Tiana has 17 oranges. How many more oranges does Tiana have than Jon?

____ ◯ ____ = ____

____ ◯ ____ = ____

Tiana has ____ more oranges than Jon.

7. ✅ Assessment Practice

Mackenzie picks some apples.

She eats 3 apples.

Now she has 9 apples.

How many apples did Mackenzie pick to start?

Ⓐ 3 apples

Ⓑ 6 apples

Ⓒ 9 apples

Ⓓ 12 apples

Activity

Solve & Share

Write a number story for 14 – 8.
Then write an equation to match your story.

I can ...
use reasoning to write and
solve number stories.

I can also add and
subtract within 20.

_____

_____

_____

Thinking Habits

What do the numbers
stand for?

_____

How can I use a word
problem to show what
an equation means?

_____

_____ – _____ = _____

Write a number story for 5 + 7.

Then write an equation to match your story.

I think about what 5, 7, and the + sign mean in the problem. I can use that to write a story.

How can I show what the numbers and symbols mean?

Lee sees 5 bugs in her garden.

Then 7 more bugs fly in. How many bugs are in her garden now?

There were 5 bugs and 7 more bugs came. So, you add.

5 + 7 = 12
Lee sees 12 bugs.

Convince Me! How would a story about 12 − 7 be alike and different from a story about 5 + 7?

☆ **Guided Practice** ☆ Complete the number story.
Then complete the equation to match the story.
Draw a picture to help.

1. 17 − 9 = _____

Carlos has __17__ dog treats.
Tom has __9__ dog treats.
How many more treats does Carlos have?

_____ more dog treats

Tools Assessment

Independent Practice   Write a number story to show the problem. Complete the equation to match your story.

2. 9 + 4 = ____

_____

_____

_____

3. 12 – 4 = ____

_____

_____

_____

4. 19 – 10 = ____

_____

_____

_____

You can use pictures, numbers, or words to help you.

School Books Jon takes 2 books home.

He leaves 4 books at school.

How can Jon write an addition story about his school books?

5. **Reasoning** Write an addition question
about Jon's books.

6. **Model** Draw a picture and write
an addition equation to solve your
addition question.

7. **Explain** Is $6 - 4 = 2$ in the same
fact family as your addition equation?

Circle **Yes** or **No.**   **Yes   No**

Use words, pictures, or equations to
explain.

Show the Word

Color these sums and differences. Leave the rest white.

| 6 | 7 | 4 |

I can ...
add and subtract within 10.

I can also be precise in my work.

9 – 5	8 – 4	1 + 3	10 – 3	4 + 3	1 + 6	7 – 1	9 – 3	5 + 1
2 + 1	6 – 2	7 – 4	5 + 2	9 – 7	7 – 0	6 – 0	6 + 2	2 + 4
8 + 2	10 – 6	2 + 6	7 + 0	6 + 3	10 – 3	4 + 2	6 + 0	10 – 4
4 + 4	3 + 1	4 – 3	8 – 1	4 + 5	6 + 1	8 – 2	2 + 1	9 + 1
8 – 7	4 + 0	6 + 4	9 – 2	3 + 4	2 + 5	3 + 3	6 – 1	6 + 3

The word is

_____ _____ _____

A-Z
Glossary

Word List
- difference
- doubles fact
- fact family
- related facts

Understand Vocabulary

1. Cross out the numbers below that do **NOT** show the difference for $18 - 8$.

16   14

11   10

2. Cross out the problems below that do **NOT** show a doubles fact.

$4 + 5$ $6 + 4$

$4 + 4$ $5 + 4$

3. Write the related fact.

$12 - 7 = 5$

___ ◯ ___ ◯ ___

4. Write the related fact.

$10 + 9 = 19$

___ ◯ ___ ◯ ___

5. Write the related fact.

$6 = 14 - 8$

___ ◯ ___ ◯ ___

Use Vocabulary in Writing

6. Write equations using the numbers shown in the model.

Then explain what the equations are called using a word from the Word List.

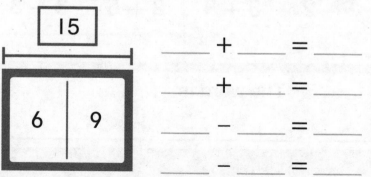

15

6 | 9

___ + ___ = ___

___ + ___ = ___

___ − ___ = ___

___ − ___ = ___

Name _____

_____

You can count back on a number line to subtract.

Find $10 - 6$.

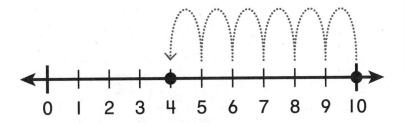

Start at 10 and count back 6 to get to 4.

$10 - 6 =$

You can also count on to subtract.

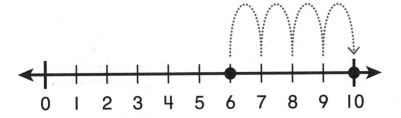

Start at 6 and count on 4 to get to 10.

$6 + 4 = 10$, so $10 - 6 = 4$.

$10 - 6 = \underline{4}$

Find the difference.
Use the number line to count back or count on.

1. Find $9 - 6$.

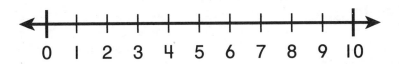

$9 - 6 =$ _____

2. Find $10 - 5$.

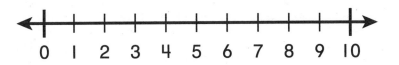

$10 - 5 =$ _____

Set B

You can make 10 to subtract.

$15 - 6 = ?$

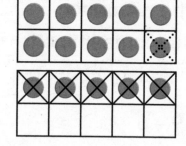

First subtract 5 from 15 to get to 10.

$15 - 5 = 10$

Then take away 1 more to get to 6.

$15 - 6 = \underline{9}$

Make 10 to subtract.
Then complete the subtraction fact.

3. $16 - 7 = \underline{}$

$16 - \underline{} = 10$

$10 - \underline{} = \underline{}$

4. $13 - 6 = \underline{}$

$13 - \underline{} = 10$

$10 - \underline{} = \underline{}$

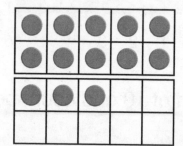

Set C

You can write a fact family to match the model.

$14 = 6 + 8$

$\underline{14} = \underline{8} + \underline{6}$

$6 = 14 - 8$

$\underline{8} = \underline{14} - \underline{6}$

14

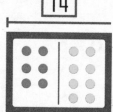

Write a fact family to match the model.

5. $\underline{} + \underline{} = \underline{}$

$\underline{} + \underline{} = \underline{}$

$\underline{} - \underline{} = \underline{}$

$\underline{} - \underline{} = \underline{}$

15

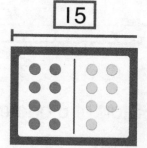

Name _____

Set D

You can use addition to help you subtract.

$15 - 7 = ?$

Think:

$7 + \underset{8}{\underline{\quad}} = 15$

The missing part is 8.

So, $15 - 7 = 8$.

15

?

Use addition to subtract. Complete the equations.

6. $13 - 8 = ?$

Think:

$8 + \underline{\quad} = 13$

So, $13 - 8 = \underline{\quad}$.

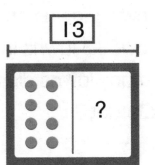

13

?

Set E

You can use different strategies to subtract $14 - 6$.

14

6 | ?

Think
Addition

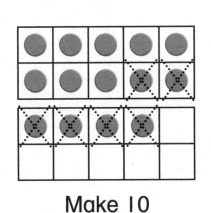

Make 10

Find each difference. Choose a strategy to use.

7.   12
      $-\ 4$
      ☐

8.   17
      $-\ 8$
      ☐

You can write an equation to show a word problem.

Jaime mows some lawns on Saturday and Sunday.
He mows 8 lawns on Sunday.
He mows 13 lawns in all.
How many lawns did Jaime mow on Saturday?

$$\underline{5} \ \bigoplus \ \underline{8} = \underline{13}$$

$\underline{5}$ lawns

9. Davis has some pens.
He gives 4 to Glenn.
Now he has 7 pens.
How many pens did Davis start with?
Write an equation to solve.
Draw a picture to help.

___ ◯ ___ = ___

___ pens

Thinking Habits

Reasoning

What do the numbers stand for?

How can I use a word problem to show what an equation means?

Write a number story for the problem. Then complete the equation.

10. $9 + 4 = $ ___

_____

_____

_____

1. Frank has 15 books to read.
He reads 9 of them.
How many books does Frank
have left to read?

_____ books

2. Mark has some red marbles. **Assessment Practice**
He has 8 blue marbles.
Mark has 13 marbles in all.
How many red marbles does
he have?

Ⓐ 4   Ⓑ 5

Ⓒ 6   Ⓓ 7

---

3. Which fact family matches the picture of the big ducks and small ducks?

$8 + 0 = 8$	$5 + 9 = 14$	$5 + 8 = 13$	$8 + 9 = 17$
$0 + 8 = 8$	$9 + 5 = 14$	$8 + 5 = 13$	$9 + 8 = 17$
$8 - 0 = 8$	$14 - 5 = 9$	$13 - 5 = 8$	$17 - 9 = 8$
$8 - 8 = 0$	$14 - 9 = 5$	$13 - 8 = 5$	$17 - 8 = 9$
Ⓐ	Ⓑ	Ⓒ	Ⓓ

4. Which related subtraction fact can be solved using $7 + 8 = 15$?

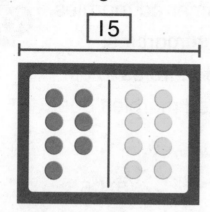

Ⓐ $15 - 8 = 7$

Ⓑ $14 - 7 = 7$

Ⓒ $8 - 7 = 1$

Ⓓ $8 - 8 = 0$

5. There are 13 birds in a tree.
Then 6 birds fly away.
How many birds are still in the tree?

Make 10 to solve.
Complete the missing numbers.

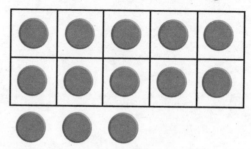

$13 - \underline{\hspace{1cm}} = 10$

$10 - \underline{\hspace{1cm}} = \underline{\hspace{1cm}}$

$13 - 6 = \underline{\hspace{1cm}}$

6. Gloria has 7 yellow pencils. She has 9 red pencils.
Which strategy would **NOT** help you find $9 - 7$?

Ⓐ Make 10

Ⓑ Think Addition

Ⓒ Count to Subtract

Ⓓ My Way

Name _____

7. Nina bakes 14 corn muffins.
She gives away 8 corn muffins.
How many are left? Write an equation
to explain.

_____ corn muffins

8. Find 16 – 7.
Write a related addition
fact to help.

16 – 7 = _____

9. Use the number line to count on or count back to find the difference.
Show your work.

12 – 4 = _____

10. Ming has 14 books. She sells 8 books.
How many books does she have left?

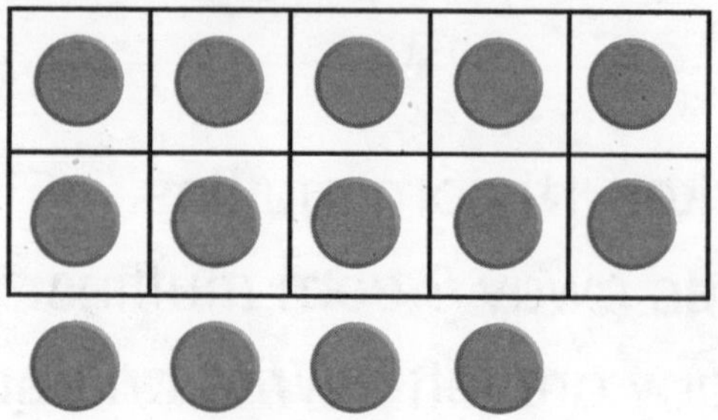

Make 10 to solve. Use counters and the ten-frame.

_____ books

11. A box has 16 skateboard parts. Maria used some of the parts.
Now there are 7 parts left.

Write a subtraction equation to show how many
parts Maria used.

_____ – _____ = _____   Maria used _____ parts.

12. Write a number story for 19 – 10.

Then write an equation to match your story and solve the problem.

_____

_____

_____

Maria's Stickers

Maria collects stickers.

The chart shows the different stickers he has.

Maria's Stickers	
Type of Sticker	**Number of Stickers**
 moon	15
cloud	7
sun	9
rainbow	8
star	12

1. How many more moon stickers than sun stickers does Maria have?

Count, make 10, or think addition to solve.

_____ more moon stickers

---

2. Maria gives some cloud stickers to Tom.
Now she has 5 cloud stickers.
How many cloud stickers did Maria give away?

Write an equation to solve the problem.

_____ ◯ _____ = _____

_____ cloud stickers

3. Complete the fact family using the number of cloud and rainbow stickers.

7   ☁   8   🌈

$$7 + 8 = 15$$

____ + ____ = ____

____ − ____ = ____

____ − ____ = ____

4. Wendy gives Maria 3 more rainbow stickers.
How many rainbow stickers does Maria have now?
Complete the equation to solve.

8 ◯ ____ = ____

____ rainbow stickers

5. Write a story to show and solve 12 − 8. Make your problem about star stickers. Draw a picture and write an equation to match your story.

_____

_____

_____

_____

_____

____ ◯ ____ = ____

Work with Addition and Subtraction Equations

Essential Question: How can adding and subtracting help you solve or complete equations?

Animals cannot speak like we do. They communicate in other ways.

Some animals that live underwater communicate using sonar.

Wow! Let's do this project and learn more.

enVision STEM Project: Underwater Communication

Find Out Talk to friends and relatives about how animals such as dolphins use sonar. Ask them to help you learn more about sonar in a book or on a computer.

Journal: Make a Book Show what you found out. In your book, also:

- Draw a picture of one way that sonar is used.

- Make up and solve addition and subtraction problems about the animals that use sonar to communicate.

Name _____

Review What You Know

Vocabulary

1. Circle the **addends** in the equation.

$$4 + 5 = 9$$

2. Circle the equation that is a **related fact** for $10 - 8 = 2$.

$$8 - 6 = 2$$

$$8 + 2 = 10$$

3. Circle the number that will complete the **fact family**.

$$3 + \underline{\ ?\ } = 10$$

$$\underline{\ ?\ } + 3 = 10$$

$$10 - 3 = \underline{\ ?\ }$$

$$10 - \underline{\ ?\ } = 3$$

8   14   7   5

Subtraction Stories

Use cubes to solve. Write the subtraction equation.

4. 8 squirrels are on the ground. 5 are eating acorns. How many squirrels are **NOT** eating acorns?

_____ – _____ = _____

5. Brett has 5 markers. Pablo has 3 markers. How many more markers does Brett have than Pablo?

_____ – _____ = _____

Related Facts

6. Write the related subtraction facts.

$$9 = 4 + 5$$

_____ = _____ – _____

_____ = _____ – _____

Name _____

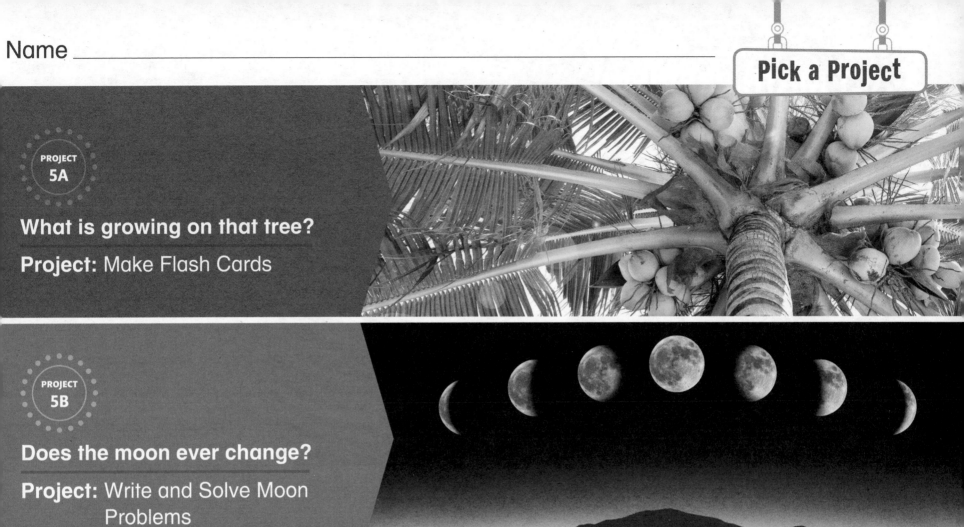

PROJECT 5A

What is growing on that tree?

Project: Make Flash Cards

PROJECT 5B

Does the moon ever change?

Project: Write and Solve Moon
Problems

PROJECT 5C

Who captured more pieces?

Project: Play a Game of Checkers

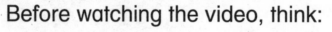

Math Modeling

Weighed Down

Video

Before watching the video, think:

What does it mean for two sides to be balanced? When it's not balanced, how do you know which side weighs more?

I can ...
model with math to solve a problem that involves making true equations.

Topic 5 | 3-Act Math

Name _____

Find the missing number in this equation:

$$7 + \underline{} = 13$$

Explain how you found the missing number.

I can ...
find the unknown number in an equation.

I can also make math arguments.

Look at this problem:

$12 - \underline{\hspace{1cm}} = 3$

This means that 12 take away some number is the same as 3.

You can use counters to find the missing number.

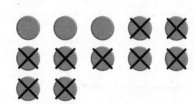

$12 - \underline{9} = 3$

You can also use addition to find the missing number.

$3 + \underline{9} = 12$,

so $12 - \underline{9} = 3$.

9 is the missing number. 9 makes the equation true.

Convince Me! What is the missing number in the equation $\underline{\hspace{1cm}} + 4 = 9$? How do you know?

☆ **Guided Practice** ☆ Write the missing numbers. Then draw or cross out counters to show your work.

1. $14 - \underline{7} = 7$

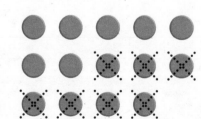

2. $4 + \underline{\hspace{1cm}} = 12$

---

214 two hundred fourteen

Topic 5 | Lesson 1

Name _____

Independent Practice   Write the missing numbers.
Draw counters to show your work.

3. ____ − 9 = 8

4. ____ = 8 + 3

5. ____ + 6 = 12

6. 8 + ____ = 15

7. 14 − ____ = 6

8. ____ = 11 − 8

9. **Number Sense** Write the missing number
to make each equation true.

9 + ____ = 19

20 = ____ + 10

____ − 10 = 9

____ − 10 = 10

How does solving one problem help you with the next?

10. Reasoning Adam wants to visit 13 states on a road trip. He has visited 7 states so far.
How many states does Adam have left to visit?

13 $\bigcirc$ ____ = ____

____ states

11. Chelsea needs to make 11 costumes in all for her dance class. She has 4 costumes left to make.
How many costumes did Chelsea already make?

11 = ____ $\bigcirc$ ____

____ costumes

12. Higher Order Thinking Find the missing number in the equation $5 + \underline{\quad} = 14$. Then write a story that matches the problem.

13. ☑ **Assessment Practice** Match each equation with the correct missing number.

17 − ____ = 7   6

____ + 6 = 12   3

4 + ____ = 13   10

____ − 1 = 2   9

Solve & Share

An equation is true if both sides are equal.

Circle the equations that are true.
Show why you think so.

Activity

Lesson 5-2
True or False Equations

I can ...
understand that the equal sign means "has the same value as."

I can also be precise in my work.

$5 = 11 - 6$

$5 + 6 = 6 + 5$

$7 = 7$

$4 + 5 = 8$

$9 + 2 = 11$

 Visual Learning A-Z Glossary

Is this equation true?

$3 + 6 = 4 + 5$

Find the value of each side of the equation.

$3 + 6$

$4 + 5$

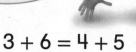 This equation is true. Both sides equal 9.

$3 + 6 = 4 + 5$

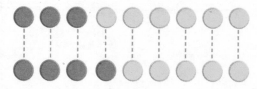

$9 = 9$

Even equations with no operation symbols can be true.

$8 = 8$ is a true statement.

Convince Me! Is the equation $4 = 11 - 6$ true? Explain.

☆ **Guided Practice** ☆ Tell if each equation is **True** or **False**. Use the counters to help you.

1. $5 + 2 = 9 - 3$

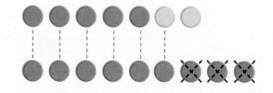

True (False)

2. $7 = 8 - 1$

True False

Name _____

Independent Practice Tell if each equation is **True** or **False**.
You can draw counters to help.

3. $5 + 5 = 6 + 4$

True   False

4. $9 = 9 - 1$

True   False

5. $3 + 3 = 11 - 8$

True   False

6. $13 - 4 = 15 - 6$

True   False

7. $7 + 7 = 12 - 5$

True   False

8. $10 + 8 = 9 + 9$

True   False

9. $7 + 3 = 10 + 2$

True   False

10. $6 + 8 = 8 + 6$

True   False

11. $4 + 2 = 6 + 1$

True   False

12. Be Precise Shawna has 8 paper airplanes. She gives away 1 plane. Frank has 5 paper airplanes and gets 2 more.

Make sure you use numbers, units, and symbols correctly. Does the equation match the story?

_____ − _____ = _____ + _____

True   False

Shawna has _____ planes.

Frank has _____ planes.

13. Higher Order Thinking Can you prove that $4 + 2 = 5 + 1$ is true without solving both sides of the equation? Explain.

_____

_____

_____

_____

_____

14. ☑ **Assessment Practice** Which equations shown below are **false**? Choose two that apply.

☐ $10 - 3 = 14 - 7$

☐ $4 + 3 = 7 + 1$

☐ $6 + 6 = 8 + 3$

☐ $17 - 8 = 9$

Name _____

Solve & Share

What number goes in the blank to make the equation true? How do you know?

I can ...
fill in the missing number in equations to make them true.

I can also be precise in my work.

$2 + 5 = \underline{} + 6$

Fill in the missing number to make this equation true.

$$10 - \underline{\quad} = 3 + 4$$

I can solve one side of the equation first. I know that $3 + 4 = 7$.

You can use counters to find the missing number.

$$10 - \underline{\quad} = 7$$

The equal sign means "the same value as," so I need to subtract something from 10 to get 7.

I took away 3 counters to get to 7, so the missing number is 3.

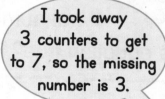

$$10 - \underline{3} = 3 + 4$$

Convince Me! What number can you write in the blank to make this equation true? Use pictures or words to show how you know.

$$8 + \underline{\quad} = 6 + 6$$

☆ **Guided Practice** ☆ Write the missing numbers to make the equations true. Draw counters to help.

1. $10 + \underline{?} = 5 + 7$

$10 + \underline{?} = 12$

$10 + \underline{2} = 12$

2. $9 - 5 = 6 - \underline{?}$

$\underline{\quad} = 6 - \underline{?}$

$\underline{\quad} = 6 - \underline{\quad}$

Topic 5 | Lesson 3

Independent Practice   Write the missing number that makes each equation true.

3. ___ $+ 6 = 4 + 9$

4. $14 - 7 =$ ___ $- 3$

5. $8 +$ ___ $= 9 + 4$

6. $10 -$ ___ $= 7 - 3$

7. $15 - 10 = 10 -$ ___

8. $7 + 4 = 8 +$ ___

9. $10 + 2 =$ ___ $+ 4$

10. $13 - 10 =$ ___ $- 7$

11. ___ $+ 7 = 9 + 1$

12. enVision® STEM Kari and Chris make "telephones" with paper cups and string. They take a piece of string that is 13 feet long and cut it into two pieces. One piece is 8 feet long. How long is the other piece of string? Write the missing number in the equations.

___ $= 13 - 8$

$13 =$ ___ $+ 8$ ___ feet

You can think about subtraction as a missing addend problem.

13. Reasoning Kim has 14 tennis balls. Danny has 4 tennis balls. How many more tennis balls does Kim have than Danny?

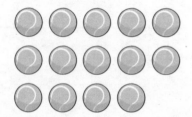

_____ ◯ _____ = _____ _____ more

14. Ron finds 10 rocks but drops 1 rock. Anson finds 3 rocks.
How many more rocks would Anson have to find to have the same number of rocks as Ron?

$10 - 1 = 3 +$ _____   _____ more

15. Higher Order Thinking José has 5 red crayons and 8 blue crayons.
Tasha has 10 red crayons and some blue crayons.
If Tasha has the same number of crayons as José, how many blue crayons does she have? Tell how you know.

_____

_____

16. ☑ Assessment Practice Draw an arrow to show which number will make the equation true.

1   2   3   4   5   6   7   8

$4 + 7 = 5 +$ _____

Name _____

Solve & Share

Carlos made stacks of 6 books, 4 books, and 6 books. How can you use addition to find the number of books in all three stacks?

Write two different equations to show how many books in all.

I can ...
find different strategies to add three numbers.

I can also look for patterns.

___ + ___ + ___ = ___

___ + ___ + ___ = ___

You can add three numbers.

$8 + 6 + 2$

Pick 2 numbers to add first.

You can make 10.

⑧ + 6 + ② = __16__

[10]

$8 + 2 = 10$
$10 + 6 = 16$

You can make a double.

$8 +$ ⑥ $+$ ② $=$ __16__

[8]

$6 + 2 = 8$
$8 + 8 = 16$

You can add any two numbers first.

③
⑤ [8]   3
+ 4   5
12   + ④
            12   [9]

The sums are the same.

Convince Me! Why can you pick any two numbers to add first when you add three numbers?

☆ **Guided Practice** ☆ Add the circled numbers first. Write their sum in the box. Then write the sum of all three numbers.

1. ② $+$ ⑨ $+ 1 =$ __12__

   [11]

   $2 +$ ⑨ $+$ ① $=$ __12__

   [10]

2. ⑥ $+$ ③ $+ 2 =$ ___

   [ ]

   $6 +$ ③ $+$ ② $=$ ___

   [ ]

Tools   Assessment

Independent Practice

Circle two numbers to add first. Write their sum in the box at the right. Then write the sum of all three numbers.

3.
```
   6
   6   ☐
 + 1
 ───
  ☐
```

4.
```
   3
   7   ☐
 + 8
 ───
  ☐
```

5.
```
   2
   8   ☐
 + 3
 ───
  ☐
```

6.
```
   7
   3   ☐
 + 3
 ───
  ☐
```

7.
```
   2
   2   ☐
 + 8
 ───
  ☐
```

8.
```
   5
   0   ☐
 + 9
 ───
  ☐
```

9. Number Sense Help Alex find the missing numbers.
The numbers on each branch add up to 15.

Remember, you can add in any order.

10. **Look for Patterns** Maya puts 7 books on a shelf and 3 books on another shelf. Then she puts 5 books on the last shelf. How many books did Maya put on all three shelves?

Can you break the problem into simpler parts?

_____ + _____ + _____ = _____

_____ books

11. **Higher Order Thinking** Explain how to add $7 + 2 + 3$. Use pictures, numbers, or words.

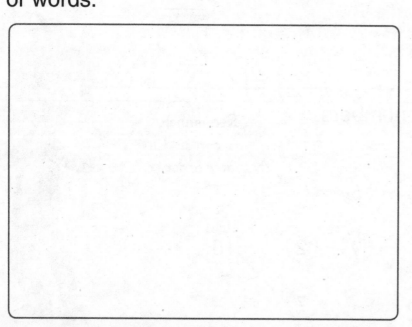

12. ☑ **Assessment Practice** Ken buys 7 pencils, 6 markers, and 4 pens. He wants to know how many items he bought in all.

Which two numbers can he add first to make a 10?

Ⓐ $7 + 6$ Ⓑ $6 + 4$

Ⓒ $7 + 4$ Ⓓ $5 + 4$

Name _____

Solve & Share

I have 6 oranges, Alex has 2 pears, and Jada has 4 apples. How many pieces of fruit do we have in all?

Write 2 different addition equations to solve the problem.

___ + ___ + ___ = ___

___ + ___ + ___ = ___

Vince collects red rocks. He separates them into 3 baskets. How many red rocks does he have in all?

 5
 4
 6

I can add 5 + 4 first and then add 6.

$5 + 4 = 9$
$9 + 6 = 15$

I can add 4 + 6 first to make 10 and then add 5.

$4 + 6 = 10$
$10 + 5 = 15$

 5
 4
 6

I can group the numbers either way. The sum is the same.

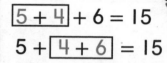

$\boxed{5 + 4} + 6 = 15$
$5 + \boxed{4 + 6} = 15$

Vince has 15 red rocks.

Convince Me! How can grouping numbers in a different way help you to solve a problem?

☆ **Guided** ☆ Write an equation to solve each problem.
Practice Choose a way to group the addends.

1. Tess finds some shells at the beach. She finds 7 pink shells, 3 black shells, and 4 white shells. How many shells does Tess find in all?

   _7_ + _3_ + _4_ = _14_   _14_ shells

2. Tom sees some birds. He sees 4 red birds, 2 blue birds, and 6 black birds. How many birds does Tom see in all?

   ___ + ___ + ___ = ___   ___ birds

Independent Practice   Write an equation to solve each problem.
Choose a way to group the addends.

3. Pat has sports cards. He has 8 baseball cards, 2 football cards, and 3 basketball cards.
How many cards does Pat have in all?

____ + ____ + ____ = ____

____ cards

4. Bob plants seeds. He plants 2 brown seeds, 6 white seeds, and 8 black seeds. How many seeds does Bob plant in all?

____ + ____ + ____ = ____

____ seeds

Write the missing numbers for each problem.

5. **Algebra** $16 = 7 + \underline{\hspace{0.5cm}} + 6$

6. **Algebra** $11 = 2 + 2 + \underline{\hspace{0.5cm}}$

7. **Vocabulary** Julio finds 3 ladybugs and some ants. Then he finds 5 beetles. Julio finds 14 bugs in all. How many ants did Julio find?
Write the missing **addend**.

$14 = 3 + \underline{\hspace{0.5cm}} + 5$

Julio found ____ ants.

8. **Higher Order Thinking** Rosa picks 12 flowers from her garden. She picks some purple flowers. Then she picks 4 pink flowers and 3 yellow flowers. How many purple flowers did Rosa pick?

$12 = ? + 4 + 3$

Rosa picked ____ purple flowers.

9. **Generalize** Dan throws 3 beanbags at the target. The numbers on the target show the score for each beanbag.

Write an addition equation to find Dan's score.

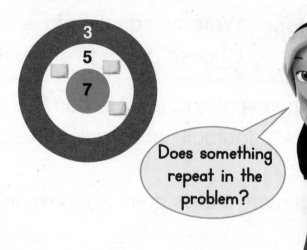

Does something repeat in the problem?

_____ + _____ + _____ = _____

10. **Higher Order Thinking** Write a story problem about toys. The story should match the addition equation below.

$4 + 1 + 9 = 14$

11. ☑ **Assessment Practice** Joy throws 3 beanbags at the target. She scores 17 points.

Which picture shows her target?

Ⓐ

Ⓑ

Ⓒ

Ⓓ

Name _____

Solve & Share

José has 5 more erasers than Lois. José has 7 erasers. How many erasers does Lois have? Write your answers below.

I can ... solve word problems involving comparisons.

I can also make sense of problems.

José's erasers

Lois's erasers

Steve has 13 books. Claire has 4 fewer books than Steve. How many books does Claire have?

You can use a bar model to show the problem.

Steve's books

13

?	4

Claire's books   **4 fewer books**

You can write an addition or subtraction equation to see how many books Claire has.

$13 - 4 = \underline{9}$

$\underline{9} + 4 = 13$

13

9	4

So, Claire has 9 books.

Convince Me! Tom made 8 fewer sandcastles than Tina. Tina made 10 sandcastles. How many sandcastles did Tom make?

☆ Guided Practice ☆ Use the model to solve the problem.

1. Sal has 8 more magazines than Gemma. Sal has 15 magazines. How many magazines does Gemma have?

Sal's magazines

15

7	8

Gemma's magazines   **8 more magazines**

$\underline{8} + \underline{7} = \underline{15}$

Gemma has ____ magazines.

Tools Assessment

Independent Practice Use the models to complete the problems.

2. Alan picks up 3 toys. Then he picks up 8 more. How many toys did Alan pick up in all?

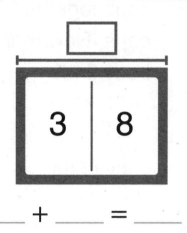

_____ + _____ = _____

Alan picked up _____ toys in all.

3. Jack makes 5 fewer fruit cups than Sandi. Sandi makes 11 fruit cups. How many fruit cups did Jack make?

11

	5

_____ − _____ = _____

Jack made _____ fruit cups.

Fill in the missing numbers for the model and the equation. Choose addition or subtraction to solve.

4. Harry has 5 fewer buttons than Tina. Harry has 7 buttons. How many buttons does Tina have?

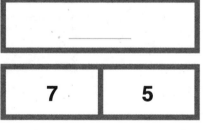

_____ ◯ _____ = _____

_____ buttons

5. Mark calls some people. Jane calls 8 people. They called 17 people in all. How many people did Mark call?

_____ ◯ _____ = _____

_____ people

6. Make Sense Ashlyn had some grapes. She gives 5 grapes to Anna. Now Ashlyn has 7 grapes. How many grapes did Ashlyn have before?

_____ ◯ _____ = _____

Ashlyn had _____ grapes before.

7. Make Sense Lucy and Tim find 15 bottle caps together. Tim finds 7 of the bottle caps. How many of the bottle caps does Lucy find?

_____ ◯ _____ = _____

Lucy finds _____ bottle caps.

8. Higher Order Thinking Draw a model to show the equation. Then write and solve the equation.

$$16 - 10 = \underline{?}$$

_____ − _____ = _____

9. ☑ Assessment Practice Tanner has 3 more pets than Ava. Tanner has 7 pets. How many pets does Ava have? Use the models to solve the problem.

7

_____	3

_____ ◯ _____ = _____

Ava has _____ pets.

Name _____

Solve & Share

Write a true equation with one number on one side and three numbers on the other side.

Each number should be different.

Explain your reasoning.

I can ...
understand that the equal sign means "the same value as" and I will use precise language when talking about it.

I can also add and subtract within 20.

Thinking Habits

Am I using numbers and symbols correctly?

Is my answer clear?

____ = ____ + ____ + ____

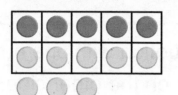

What missing number can you write to make the equation true?

$14 = 5 + \underline{} + 8$

The equal sign means "the same value as."

How can I be precise as I solve this problem?

I can use words, numbers, and symbols correctly.

14 has the same value as 5 plus 8 plus some number.

$5 + 8 = 13$,
so $14 = 13 + \underline{1}$.

$13 + 1 = 14$,
so 1 is the missing number.

$14 = 5 + \underline{1} + 8$

Convince Me! Is the equation below true or false? How do you know?

$10 + 5 = 9 + 3 + 3$

✫ Guided Practice ✫ Write the symbol (+, −, or =) or number to make the equation true. Then tell how you know you found the correct symbol or number.

1. $3 + 8 = 4 + \boxed{7}$

2. $4 + 3 + \boxed{} = 13$

Tools Assessment

Independent Practice

Write the symbol (+, −, or =) or number to make the equation true.
Then tell how you know you found the correct symbol or number.

3. 19 ◯ 10 = 9

_____

_____

_____

4. 20 = ☐ + 5 + 5

_____

_____

_____

5. 10 + 1 ◯ 6 + 5

_____

_____

_____

6. 9 − 2 = 10 ◯ 3

_____

_____

_____

7. Algebra Write the missing number in the equation below. Explain how you know.

42 + 55 = 55 + ☐

_____

_____

Think about the meanings of the symbols.

Balloon Party Dani has 7 green and 4 yellow balloons. Gene has 15 blue balloons.

8. **Explain** If Gene gives 4 of his balloons away, then he and Dani will have the same number. Fill in the blanks to make the equation true. Use +, −, or =.

7 ◯ 4 ◯ 15 ◯ 4

Explain how you chose the symbols.

_____

_____

_____

_____

How do you know the equation is true?

_____

_____

_____

9. **Be Precise** If Gene keeps all 15 blue balloons, how many balloons would Dani need to buy to have the same number as Gene? Complete the equation to find the answer.

7 ◯ 4 ◯ ___ ◯ 15

Did you use numbers and symbols correctly? Explain how you know.

_____

_____

_____

Name _____

Point & Tally

Find a partner. Get paper and a pencil.

Each partner chooses a different color: light blue or dark blue.

Partner 1 and Partner 2 each point to a black number at the same time. Subtract Partner 1's number from Partner 2's number.

If the answer is on your color, you get a tally mark.

Work until one partner gets twelve tally marks.

I can …
add and subtract within 10.

I can also make math arguments.

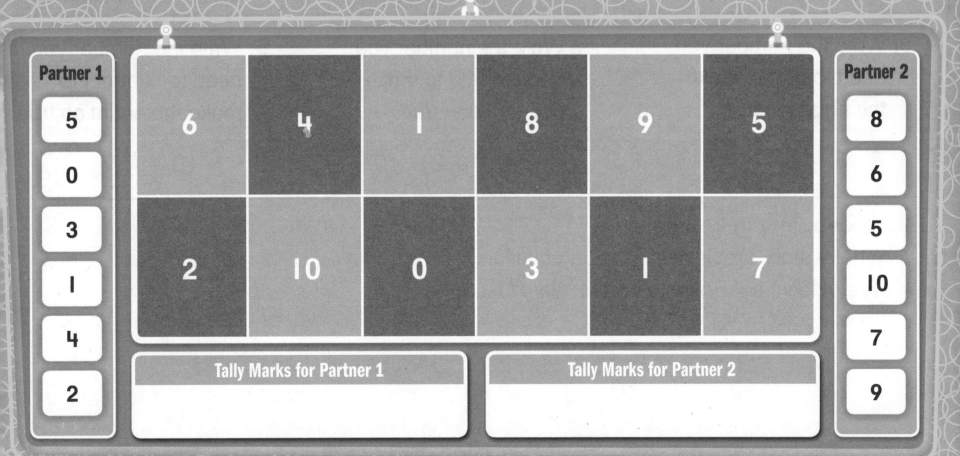

Partner 1							Partner 2
5	6	4	1	8	9	5	8
0							6
3							5
1	2	10	0	3	1	7	10
4							7
2							9

Tally Marks for Partner 1

Tally Marks for Partner 2

Glossary

Word List
- add
- equation
- more
- subtract

Understand Vocabulary

1. Circle **True** or **False** for the addition equation below.

$$4 + 6 = 5 + 2 + 3$$

True　　　　　　　False

2. Circle **True** or **False** for the subtraction equation below.

$$10 = 11 - 2$$

True　　　　　　　False

3. Write the number you need to add to make the equation true.

$$7 - 3 = 2 + \underline{\quad}$$

4. Write the number you need to add to make the equation true.

$$\underline{\quad} + 4 + 2 = 10$$

5. Write the number you need to subtract to make the equation true.

$$9 = 10 - \underline{\quad}$$

Use Vocabulary in Writing

6. Write a story problem with a true equation. Use at least two words from the Word List.

Name _____

Set A

Solve to find out if the equation is **True** or **False**.

$$6 + 5 = 3 + 8$$

Solve one side first. $6 + 5 = 11$
Solve the other side. $3 + 8 = 11$

$$11 = 11$$

This equation is **True**.

Tell whether each equation is **True** or **False**.

1. $8 - 5 = 4 + 1$

   True   **False**

2. $3 + 1 = 12 - 8$

   True   **False**

Set B

Write the missing numbers to make the equations true.

$4 + 7 = 6 + \underline{}$

Both sides should be equal.

$4 + 7 = 11$

So, $6 + \underline{5} = 11$.

The missing number is 5.

$4 + 7 = 6 + \underline{5}$

Find and write the missing numbers to make the equations true.

3. $11 = \underline{} + 4$

4. $\underline{} - 4 = 5$

5. $10 + 5 = 6 + \underline{}$

6. $9 - \underline{} = 13 - 10$

7. $14 - \underline{} = 2 + 2$

You can add three numbers in any order. $2 + 8 + 2 =$ ___?___

Make a 10. Then add 2.

$(2) + (8) + 2 = \underline{12}$

Make a double. Then add 8.

$(2) + 8 + (2) = \underline{12}$

Find the sum. Solve in any order.

8. $5 + 5 + 4 =$ _____

9. $9 + 5 + 1 =$ _____

10. $6 + 4 + 4 =$ _____

11. $3 + 3 + 5 =$ _____

Thinking Habits

Precision

Am I using numbers and symbols correctly?

Am I adding and subtracting accurately?

Write the symbol (+, −, or =) or number to make the equation true. Then tell how you know you chose the correct symbol or number.

12. $10 - 5 = 2 \bigcirc 3$

_____

_____

_____

13. $4 + 5 = 10 \bigcirc 1$

_____

_____

 Topic 5 | Reteaching

Name _____

1. A. Complete the model. Then write the missing number in the equation.

14 = _____ + 9

B. The sum in the equation has increased by 3 to give 17 = [ ] + 9.
What is the missing number?

17 = _____ + 9

2. A. Which number is missing?

16 − __?__ = 2 + 6

Ⓐ 10

Ⓑ 9

Ⓒ 8

Ⓓ 7

B. Write the missing numbers to make each equation true.

16 − _____ = 2 + 7

16 − _____ = 2 + 8

16 − _____ = 2 + 9

3. Tell if the equation is **True** or **False**.

4 + 7 = 13 − 3

True   **False**

4. Tasha has 2 dogs and 3 cats. How many more pets does Tasha need if she wants a total of 11 pets?

_____ more pets

5. Bill has 10 apples. He uses 8 of them to make muffins. Josh has 6 apples. How many should he use so he has the same number as Bill?

$$10 - 8 = 6 - \underline{\quad}$$

_____ apples

6. Kerry, Tom, and Nicole want to play tennis. Kerry has 5 tennis balls. Tom has 5 tennis balls. How many tennis balls does Nicole have if they have 13 tennis balls in all?

Ⓐ 3

Ⓑ 4

Ⓒ 5

Ⓓ 6

7. In a soccer game, Andrew scores 3 fewer goals than Elsie. Elsie scores 9 goals. How many goals did Andrew score?
Complete the bar diagram and write an equation to match the story.

9

_____	3

_____ ◯ _____ = _____

_____ goals

8. Write the missing symbol (+, −, or =) to make the equation true. Use precise math language to explain how you chose the symbol.

$$16 = 4 + 8 \bigcirc 4$$

_____

_____

_____

Name _____

A Vase of Flowers

Terry and his brother, Dave, put flowers in a vase for their mother.

5 Roses

5 Daisies

2 Carnations

8 Lilies

1. Complete the equation below to show the number of lilies and roses. Use numbers and symbols (+, −, =).

   _____ + 5 ◯ _____

✓ **Performance Task**

2. How many roses, daisies, and carnations are in the vase?

   Write an equation to solve.

   _____ + _____ + _____ = _____

   Explain how you added.
   Use pictures, numbers, or words.

3. Terry puts the roses and the daisies in the vase. Dave puts the carnations and the lilies in the vase. Did they put an equal number of flowers in the vase?

Complete the equation.

_____ + _____ = _____ + _____

Fill in the missing numbers.

Terry puts _____ flowers in the vase.

Dave puts _____ flowers in the vase.

Did Terry and Dave each put an equal number of flowers in the vase?
Circle **Yes** or **No**.

Yes   **No**

4. Dave says there are 3 more daisies than carnations. What equation can he use to find out if he is right?

5 ◯ _____ ◯ _____

5. Terry says that if there were 2 fewer lilies, then the number of lilies would be equal to the number of daisies. He writes the equation below. Is this equation true or false? Explain how you know.

$8 - 2 = 5$

_____

_____

6. Terry and Dave buy more carnations. Now they have 10 in all. How many carnations did they buy? Complete the equation using +, −, or =.

10 ◯ 2 ◯ 8 _____ more carnations

Use precise math language to explain how you chose the symbols.

_____

_____

_____

TOPIC 6
Represent and Interpret Data

Essential Question: What are some ways you can collect, show, and understand data?

There are many different types of telephones.

The first telephone was invented over 100 years ago.

Wow! Let's do this project and learn more.

Digital Resources

Interactive Student Edition   Activity   Visual Learning   Video   Practice

Assessment   Games   Tools   Glossary

enVision STEM Project: Different Types of Phones

Find Out Talk to friends and relatives about the types of phones they use. Ask how phones have changed in their lifetimes.

Journal: Make a Book Show what you found out. In your book, also:

• Draw pictures of more than one type of phone. Which phone do you think is better for making calls?

• Collect data about the types of phones people use.

Name _____

Review What You Know

1. Circle the cubes that make the **equation** true.

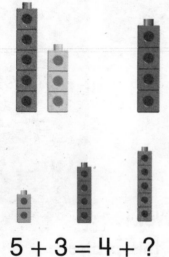

$$5 + 3 = 4 + \text{?}$$

2. Write the numbers that tell how many pieces of fruit. Then circle the group with **fewer**.

_____   _____

_ _ _ _   _ _ _ _

_____   _____

3. Write the numbers that tell how many balls. Then circle the group with **more**.

_____   _____

_ _ _ _   _ _ _ _

_____   _____

Find the Missing Part

4. Write the number that will make the equation true.

$$15 - 8 = \underline{\quad} + 1$$

5. Write each missing number.

$$5 + 3 + 2 = \underline{\quad}$$

$$9 + \underline{\quad} + 7 = 17$$

Near Doubles Facts

6. Write the missing number to solve this near doubles fact.

$$7 + \underline{\quad} = 15$$

PROJECT 6A

Which dog is your favorite?

Project: Create a Pet Data Display

PROJECT 6B

Is all art the same?

Project: Make an Art Poster

What do you like to wear?

Project: Draw an Outfit

What can shells on the beach look like?

Project: Model Favorite Seashells

Activity

Solve & Share

Judy wants to show a friend how many crayons she has of each color. How can she show this? Show one way.

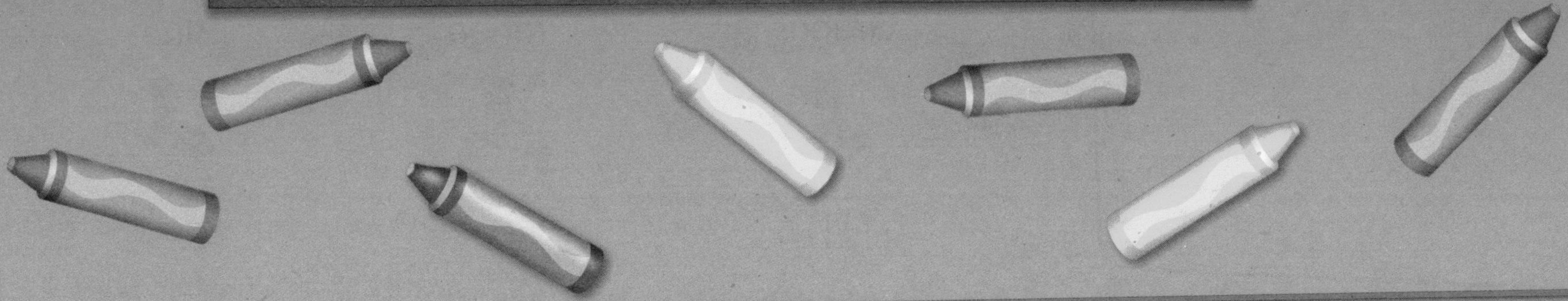

I can ... organize data into categories.

I can also model with math.

These are **tally marks**.

There are 3 tally marks.

Each tally mark stands for 1 piece of information.

Count the tally marks by 5s.

There are 20. Each 卌 stands for 5 pieces of information.

m a t h e m a t i c s
Make tally marks to show how many letters are black.

There are 6 black letters.

You can put the **data** in a **tally chart**.

Black	Red	Blue
卌 I	III	II

Convince Me! How can a tally chart help you with data you collect?

Guided Practice In the chart, make tally marks to show how many socks there are for each color.

1.

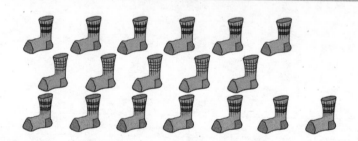

Green	Orange	Blue
		🧦
卌 I		

Name _____

Independent Practice ✩ Use the tally chart from Guided Practice to answer each question.

2. Which color sock has the most tally marks?

_____

3. How many blue socks are there?

_____ blue socks

4. How many socks are there in all?

_____ socks

Use the tally chart below to answer each question.

Saul's Closet

Shirts	Shorts	Shoes
![shirt]	![shorts]	![shoe]
卌 II	IIII	II

5. How many shorts does Saul have?

_____ shorts

6. Which item in his closet does Saul have the most of?

_____

7. enVision® STEM Rita recorded data about different types of shoes. She made a tally mark each month for each shoe until that type of shoe wore out.
Which type of shoe lasted the longest? How many months before it wore out?

Number of Months

Sneakers	Sandals	Loafers
![sneakers]	![sandals]	![loafers]
IIII	II	卌

8. Draw tally marks to show how many hats there are of each color.

Blue	Green	Purple

9. Be Precise How do you know that purple caps are shown the least?

_____

_____

Think about the definition of *least*.

_____

_____

10. Higher Order Thinking Write and answer your own question about the tally chart you made in Item 8.

_____

_____

_____

11. ☑ Assessment Practice Use the tally chart you made in Item 8. Which two sentences are true?

☐ There are 12 blue caps.

☐ There are 7 green caps.

☐ There are 3 purple caps.

☐ There are 12 caps in all.

Activity

Lesson 6-2

Collect and Represent Data

I can ...
collect information and organize it using a picture graph.

I can also model with math.

Solve & Share

What is your favorite activity to do outside?

Ask several classmates to choose Jump Rope, Basketball, or Ride a Bike. Complete the tally chart to show your data. Then answer the questions.

Favorite Outside Activity	
Jump Rope	
Basketball	
Ride a Bike	

1. Which activity has the least votes? _____

2. Which activity has the most votes? _____

Joey asks 9 friends a **survey** question.

> Which is your favorite sport to play? Basketball, soccer, or baseball?

Joey makes 1 tally mark to show what each friend says.

Favorite Sport

🏀	Basketball	III
⚽	Soccer	||||I
⚾	Baseball	I

Joey uses the data in the tally chart to make a **picture graph**.

Favorite Sport

🏀 Basketball	🏀	🏀	🏀		
⚽ Soccer	⚽	⚽	⚽	⚽	⚽
⚾ Baseball	⚾				

> Look at the picture graph! Soccer has the most votes.

Convince Me! Look at the **Favorite Sport** picture graph above. What sport do Joey's friends like least? How do you know?

☆**Guided Practice**☆ Kurt asks his friends a survey question. Use the data he collected to make a picture graph.

I.

Favorite Fruit

Pear	Banana	Apple
🍐	🍌	🍎
||||I III	III	||||I

Favorite Fruit

🍐 Pear	🍐	🍐	🍐	🍐	🍐	🍐	🍐	
🍌 Banana								
🍎 Apple								

Topic 6 | Lesson 2

Name _____

Independent Practice Use the data in the tally chart to make a picture graph. Then answer each question.

2. Favorite Rainy Day Activity

Games	Paint	Read
𝍫𝍫 II	III	𝍫𝍫 I

Favorite Rainy Day Activity

Games								
Paint								
Read								

3. Which activity is the favorite?

_____

4. How many students chose Read?

_____ students

5. Higher Order Thinking Look at the picture graph you made for Item 2. Write two sentences that are true about the data.

_____

_____

_____

6. **Model** Gina asks her friends a survey question. Then she makes a tally chart to show their favorite music instrument. Use her data to make a picture graph.

Favorite Music Instrument

Guitar	Drum	Flute
🎸	🥁	🎵
卌 I	III	IIII

Favorite Music Instrument

🎸 Guitar						
🥁 Drum						
🎵 Flute						

7. **Higher Order Thinking** How many students voted in all? _____ students

Write an equation to show your answer.

_____ = _____ + _____ + _____

8. ☑**Assessment Practice** Which musical instrument has the most votes?

Ⓐ Guitar

Ⓑ Piano

Ⓒ Flute

Ⓓ Drum

9. ☑**Assessment Practice** How many students chose the flute?

Ⓐ 5 students

Ⓑ 4 students

Ⓒ 3 students

Ⓓ 2 students

Name _____

 Activity

Lesson 6-3
Interpret Data

Solve & Share

12 students were asked, "Which vegetable do you like more at lunch, corn or peas?" This list shows their answers.

Complete the tally chart and picture graph to show the data. What do these data tell you about what students like?

I can …
interpret organized data.

I can also be precise in my work.

Favorite Lunchtime Vegetable	
Corn	
Peas	

Corn	Corn
Peas	Corn
Peas	Peas
Corn	Peas
Peas	Corn
Corn	Corn

Favorite Lunchtime Vegetable										
Corn										
Peas										

The picture graph shows how many students like milk, water, or juice with lunch.

What does the graph tell you about what students like to drink at lunch?

Lunch Drinks						
Milk						
Water						
Juice						

I can count and compare what drinks students like.

6 students like milk.
3 students like juice.
Only 1 student likes water.

So, the graph tells me that students like milk better than juice or water with lunch.

Convince Me! What other information do you know about what students like to drink at lunch?

Guided Practice Use the picture graph above to answer the questions.

1. How many more students like milk than juice?

   3 more students

2. How many fewer students like water than milk?

   _____ fewer students

3. How many more students like juice than water?

   _____ more students

Topic 6 | Lesson 3

Independent Practice ☆   Use the data in the tally chart to answer each question.

4. Use the data in the tally chart to make a picture graph.

Our Favorite Colors

Red ⬅	Blue ⬅	Purple ⬅
IIII	ЖІ II	ЖІ III

5. How many more students like purple than red?

_____ more students

_____

6. Which color is the favorite of the most students?

_____

Our Favorite Colors

⬅											
⬅											
⬅											

7. Algebra 2 students changed their vote from blue to red. Use this equation to determine how many fewer students like red than purple.

_____ + 6 = 8

_____ fewer students

8. Higher Order Thinking Write and answer a question about the data in the picture graph.

_____

_____

9. Look at the tally chart.

Our Pets

Dogs	Cats	Fish
🐕	🐈	🐠
卌 I	III	II

How many friends have dogs
for pets? _____

How many friends have fish
for pets? _____

10. **Be Precise** Look at
the picture graph.

How many more
friends have dogs
than fish? _____

How many fewer
friends have cats
than dogs or fish?

_____

Think about the
meaning of *more*
and *fewer*.

Our Pets

Dogs	Cats	Fish
🐕		
🐕		
🐕		
🐕	🐈	
🐕	🐈	🐠
🐕	🐈	🐠
🐕	🐈	🐠

11. **Higher Order Thinking** Look at the
tally chart in Item 9. How many friends
have pets? Write an equation to show
your work.

_____

_____

_____

12. ☑ **Assessment Practice** Which
question **CANNOT** be answered by
looking at the graph in Item 10?

Ⓐ How many friends have cats?

Ⓑ How many friends have hamsters?

Ⓒ How many fewer friends have fish
than dogs?

Ⓓ How many more friends have dogs
than cats?

Activity

Solve & Share

At the park, Susan sees 13 animals in all. 9 are birds. The rest are rabbits. How can Susan complete the table to show this? Show your work.

I can …
use a picture graph to interpret data.

I can also reason about math.

Birds	Rabbits

Abby asks 12 students if they like broccoli or carrots better.

5 choose broccoli.
The rest choose carrots.

How many students chose carrots?

I can count up to 12. So, 7 students chose carrots.

Use a tally chart to find the missing data.

Broccoli	Carrots
ℍℍ	ℍℍℍ

How many more or fewer students chose carrots than broccoli?

You can make a picture graph or write an equation to compare.

2 more students chose carrots.

Favorite Vegetable

| Broccoli | 🥦 🥦 🥦 🥦 🥦 | |
| Carrots | 🥕 🥕 🥕 🥕 🥕 🥕 🥕 |

$7 - 5 = \underline{2}$

Convince Me! How did Abby know to count up from 5 to 12 in the problem above?

Guided Practice Draw the missing symbols in the picture graph. Then use the graph to solve the problem.

1.

Favorite Fruit

| Apple | 🍎 🍎 🍎 | |
| Orange | 🍊 🍊 🍊 🍊 🍊 🍊 |

Jim asks 9 members of his family for their favorite fruit.

6 people say they like oranges. The rest say they like apples.

How many people say they like apples? _____ people

Topic 6 | Lesson 4

Name _____

Independent Practice Use the graphs to answer the questions. Fill in the missing data.

2. A shelf at a store holds 11 stuffed animals. There are 5 stuffed bears and the rest are stuffed penguins.

   How many stuffed penguins are on the shelf?

Sylvie's Stuffed Animals								
Bears								
Penguins								

_____ stuffed penguins

3. Zach plays 17 games in a season. 9 of the games are soccer games and the rest are baseball.

   How many baseball games does Zach play in one season?

Zach's Games									
Baseball									
Soccer									

_____ baseball games

4. **Number Sense** Jen's class makes a graph about two of their favorite kinds of movies.

   How many students took the survey?

   _____ students

Favorite Kind of Movie	
Funny	Scary

5. Reasoning Jaime makes a weather graph. He forgets to record 3 sunny days. Were there more sunny or cloudy days?

_____

Weather							
Sunny	☀	☀	☀	☀			
Cloudy	☁	☁	☁	☁	☁	☁	

6. Higher Order Thinking Ryan asks 20 students which subject is their favorite. He did not record responses for the students that chose Science.

Draw the missing tally marks. Explain how you know you drew the right number.

Reading	Math	Science	Social Studies
ⅢⅡ	ⅢⅡ ⅠⅠⅠ		ⅠⅠⅠ

_____

7. ☑ Assessment Practice Daisi asks 9 students if they like cats or dogs better. 4 choose cats. The rest choose dogs.

How many chose dogs? Help Daisi finish her graph.

Favorite Animal							
Cat	🐱	🐱	🐱	🐱			
Dog	🐶	🐶	🐶				

_____ students

Name _____

Solve & Share

Kelly asks 12 students if they like octopuses, whales, or sharks best. The tally chart shows their responses.

How many students would need to change their vote from whales to sharks to make sharks the favorite? Complete the new chart to explain.

I can …
persevere to solve problems about sets of data.

I can also add and subtract using data.

Octopuses	Whales	Sharks
|||	⊞||	||

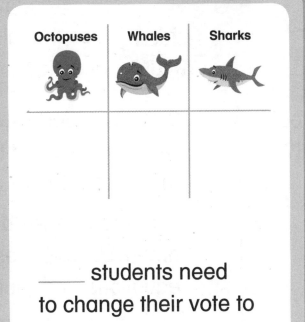

Octopuses	Whales	Sharks

_____ students need to change their vote to sharks.

Thinking Habits

What do I need to find?

What do I know?

Sarah asks 15 people if they like football or baseball. 1 more person chose football than chose baseball.

How many people chose each sport? What would the tally chart look like?

What's my plan for solving this problem?

I can...
• think about what I know.
• think about what I need to find.

Think of different ways you know to add up to 15.

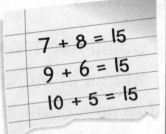

$7 + 8 = 15$
$9 + 6 = 15$
$10 + 5 = 15$

7 plus 8 equals 15, and 8 is 1 more than 7.

So, 8 people chose football and 7 people chose baseball.

Favorite Sport

Baseball	Football

Convince Me! For the survey above, why couldn't 9 choose football and 6 choose baseball?

Guided Practice Use the tally chart to answer the question.

1. 3 more students take the survey. Now, football and baseball have the same number of votes.

How many votes does each have? Use pictures, words, or equations to explain.

Favorite Sport

Baseball	Football

_____

_____

Topic 6 | Lesson 5

Independent Practice ☆ Use the chart and graph to solve the problems below.

Linzie asks 18 students if they like milk, water, or juice with lunch. 7 students like milk. 3 students like water. The rest of the students like juice.

Lunch Drinks

Milk	Water	Juice
‖‖ ‖	‖‖	

2. How many students like juice? Complete Linzie's tally chart to solve.

_____ students like juice.

3. What is the favorite drink?

_____

4. The next day Linzie asks the same question again. 3 students change their response from juice to water. What is the favorite drink now?

_____

5. Ⓐ-Ⓩ **Vocabulary** Linzie records her new **survey** results in the picture graph below.

Complete the graph to show how many students like juice.

Lunch Drinks

Milk	🥛	🥛	🥛	🥛	🥛	🥛	🥛	
Water	🧴	🧴	🧴	🧴	🧴	🧴		
Juice								

Draw pictures to show the data!

Going to School

Ebony asks 14 classmates if they take the bus, walk, or ride in a car to school.

4 students ride in a car. The same number of the remaining students take the bus or walk to school.

Going to School

Bus	Walk	Ride
		‖‖

6. **Make Sense** How can you find out how many students take the bus or walk to school?

_____

_____

_____

7. **Model** Complete the tally chart to show how Ebony's classmates voted. Write an equation to show how many walk and take the bus.

8. **Explain** How do you know your answers are correct? Use pictures, words, or equations to explain.

_____

_____

_____

Find a Match

Find a partner. Point to a clue. Read the clue.
Look below the clues to find a match. Write
the clue letter in the box next to the match.
Find a match for every clue.

I can ...
add and subtract within 10.

I can also make
math arguments.

Clues

A $4 + 6$

B $8 - 2$

C $3 - 1$

D $10 - 5$

E $8 + 1$

F $3 + 4$

G $8 - 7$

H $1 + 3$

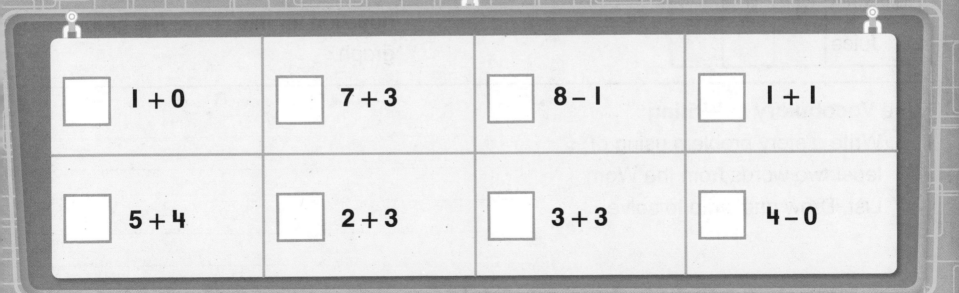

☐ $1 + 0$ ☐ $7 + 3$ ☐ $8 - 1$ ☐ $1 + 1$

☐ $5 + 4$ ☐ $2 + 3$ ☐ $3 + 3$ ☐ $4 - 0$

Vocabulary Review

A-Z
Glossary

Word List
- data
- picture graph
- survey
- tally chart
- tally marks

Understand Vocabulary

Circle the correct answer for each question using the image at the left.

Blue	Red	Green
IIII	III	ЖI

1. Green shows ____ tally marks.

    3   4   5   6

2. The image is called a _____.

    picture graph   tally chart   survey   tally mark

Fill in the blanks using words from the Word List.

Favorite Drinks

Milk	🥛	🥛	
Juice	🧃	🧃	🧃

3. This graph is called a

_____.

4. "What is your favorite drink?" could be the

_____

question for this graph.

5. You can use the

_____

to answer questions about the graph.

Use Vocabulary in Writing

6. Write a story problem using at least two words from the Word List. Draw and write to solve.

Name _____

Set A _____

You can collect and sort data into a tally chart.

Jimmy asks 10 friends what meal takes the longest to eat.

Longest Meal

Breakfast	Lunch	Dinner
III	I	JHT I

Each tally mark is one friend's answer.

The picture graph shows Jimmy's data using objects.

Longest Meal

Breakfast	▨	▨	▨			
Lunch	▨					
Dinner	▨	▨	▨	▨	▨	▨

Each ▨ is one friend's answer.

___3___ friends said breakfast was their longest meal.

Use the data from Jimmy's survey to solve each problem.

1. How many friends said dinner was their longest meal?

_____ friends

2. How many friends said breakfast or dinner was their longest meal?

_____ friends

Write an equation to answer each question.

3. How many more friends chose breakfast than lunch?

_____ − _____ = _____   _____ more

4. How many more chose dinner than breakfast?

_____ − _____ = _____   _____ more

You can use data in a picture graph to ask and answer questions.

Mari asks 16 of her friends for their favorite activity. She records their answers in a picture graph.

Favorite Activity

Soccer	⚽ ⚽ ⚽ ⚽		
Tennis	🎾 🎾 🎾 🎾 🎾 🎾 🎾	
Running	👟 👟 👟 👟 👟	

Thinking Habits

Make Sense and Persevere

What are the amounts?

What am I trying to find?

Use Mari's picture graph to answer each question.

5. How many people chose soccer or running?

_____ – _____ = _____ OR _____ + _____ = _____

6. Mari asks some more friends and they all chose tennis as their favorite activity.

Now the number of students who like tennis is the same as the number of students who like soccer or running.

How many more friends did Mari ask?

_____ more

Explain how you know.

_____

_____

_____

Name _____

1. **A.** Which set of tally marks shows the number of hats in the picture graph?

🧢 Hat	🧢	🧢	🧢	🧢
🥊 Mitt	🥊	🥊		

Ⅱ   ⅢⅠ   卌   卌Ⅰ

Ⓐ   Ⓑ   Ⓒ   Ⓓ

B. How many more mitts need to be added to have more mitts than hats?

0   Ⅰ   2   3

Ⓐ   Ⓑ   Ⓒ   Ⓓ

---

2. Use the picture graph to answer the questions.

A. Which of the following statements are true? Choose three that apply.

☐ There are 2 more penguins than bears.

☐ There are 2 fewer bears than penguins.

☐ There are more bears than penguins.

☐ There are 8 bears and penguins.

☐ There are 5 more bears than penguins.

Zoo Animals					
🐧 Penguin	🐧	🐧	🐧	🐧	🐧
🐻 Bear	🐻	🐻	🐻		

B. A third animal gets added. There are 2 giraffes. How many more penguins are there than giraffes? Write an equation that explains your answer.

Use the tally chart to solve each problem below.

3. A. Kyla asks her friends a survey question. Which is the favorite winter activity of the most students?

_____

B. How many more tally marks does skating need to have the most tally marks?
Use an equation to explain your answer.

_____

Favorite Winter Activity

🛼	Skating	Ⅲ̶Ⅼ̶
〜	Skiing	|||
🛷	Sledding	|||||||

4. A. Use the tally chart from Item 3 to complete the picture graph.

B. How many students took the survey?
Write an equation to show your work.

__ ◯ __ ◯ __ = __

____ students

Favorite Winter Activity						
🛼 Skating	🛼	🛼	🛼	🛼	🛼	
〜 Skiing						
🛷 Sledding						

Name _____

Dinosaur Project Ms. Johnson's class is doing a dinosaur project. The tally chart shows which dinosaurs the students chose.

1. How many more students chose T-Rex than Triceratops? Explain how you know. Use pictures, numbers, or words.

Dinosaur Project

Triceratops	T-Rex	Apatosaurus
卌 IIII	卌 卌 II	卌 II

2. Two students were absent when the class made the tally chart. They chose their dinosaur the next day. Ms. Johnson said that now two dinosaurs had the same number. Which dinosaur did the 2 students choose? How do you know?

_____ more students

3. Ms. Bee's class is also doing a dinosaur project. The tally chart shows which dinosaurs the students chose.

The students will draw their dinosaurs on the picture graph below when they finish their reports.

Fill in the picture graph to show what it will look like when all the reports are finished.

Dinosaur Project

Triceratops	T-Rex	Apatosaurus
𝍸𝍸𝍸 |||	𝍸𝍸𝍸 ||||	𝍸𝍸𝍸	

4. How many students still need to finish a report on the T-Rex? How many need to finish a report on the Apatosaurus? Use pictures, words, or equations to explain.

Topic 6 | Performance Task

Extend the Counting Sequence

Essential Question: How can you use what you already know about counting to count past 100?

Digital Resources

Interactive Student Edition   Activity   Visual Learning   Video   Practice

Assessment   Games   Tools   Glossary

All babies do different things to help themselves survive.

They might cry or make noise to let their parents know that they need something.

Wow! Let's do this project and learn more.

enVision STEM Project: Parents and Babies

Find Out Talk to friends and relatives about different types of animal parents and babies. Ask for help finding information about how babies communicate with their parents.

Journal: Make a Book Show what you found out. In your book, also:

- Draw how animal parents protect babies and how animal babies communicate with parents.
- Go outside or to the zoo and count animal parents and babies. How high can you count?

Name _____

Review What You Know

Vocabulary

1. Circle the number that is the **sum** in the equation.

   $17 = 9 + 8$

2. Write the **parts** shown in the model.

   8

   _____ + _____

3. Circle the word that tells which part is missing.

   $7 + \underline{\quad ? \quad} = 17$

   sum

   equals

   addend

Word Problems

4. Margie finds 7 rocks. Kara finds 6 rocks. How many rocks did they find in all?

   _____ rocks

5. Tom has 6 toy cars. Jane has some toy cars. They have 11 toy cars in all. How many toy cars does Jane have?

   _____ toy cars

The Missing Number

6. Find the missing number to solve this addition fact.

   _____ $= 10 + 5$

Name _____

PROJECT
7A

Where do you see stickers?

Project: Sing a Sticker Song

PROJECT
7B

When do you keep score?

Project: Make a Scoring Model

PROJECT
7C

How did they make that?

Project: Make a Quilt Poster

Math Modeling

Super Selfie

Video

Before watching the video, think:

Have you ever tried to print something bigger than a single piece of paper? What happens if you print something that doesn't fit on one page? What does it look like?

I can ...

model with math to solve a problem that involves counting and skip counting.

Name _____

Solve & Share

Alex put counters in some ten-frames. How can you find out how many counters there are without counting each one?

Write the number.

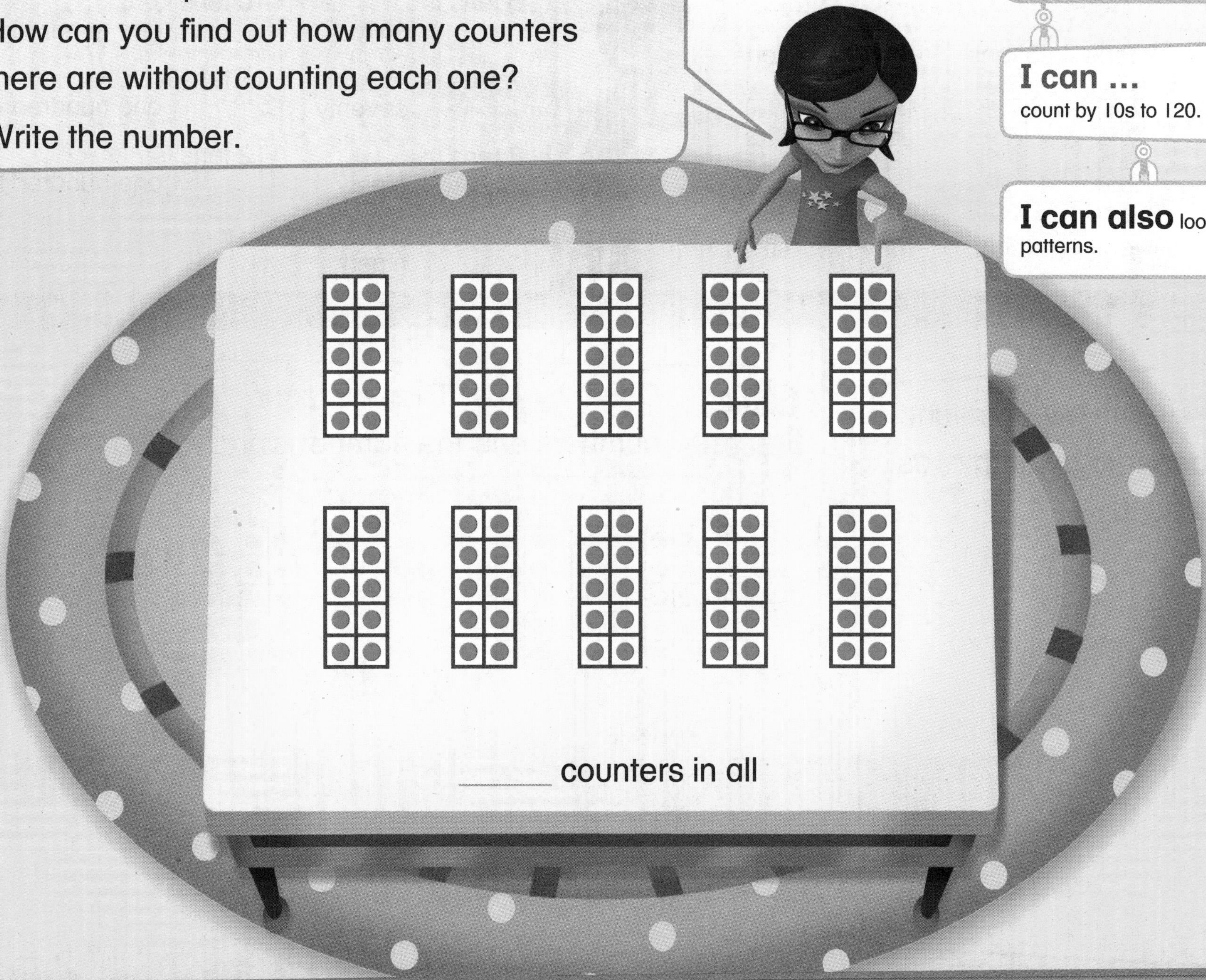

_____ counters in all

How can you count to 50 by 10s?

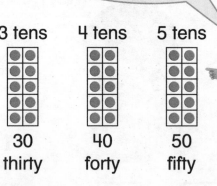

I can use ten-frames to count by 10s!

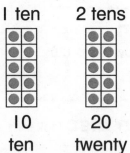

1 ten	2 tens	3 tens	4 tens	5 tens
10	20	30	40	50
ten	twenty	thirty	forty	fifty

You can also follow the pattern to count by 10s.

6 tens is __60__.   10 tens is __100__.
     sixty   one hundred

7 tens is __70__.   11 tens is __110__.
     seventy   one hundred ten

8 tens is __80__.   12 tens is __120__.
     eighty   one hundred twenty

9 tens is __90__.
     ninety

Convince Me! When might it be better to count by 10s instead of by 1s?

Guided Practice Count by 10s. Then write the numbers and the number word.

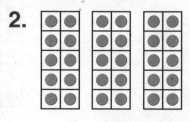

1. ___4___ tens is __40__.
forty

2. _____ tens is _____.

Topic 7 | Lesson

Independent Practice   Count by 10s. Write the numbers and the number word.

3.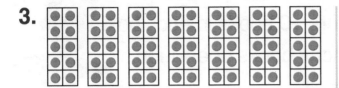

_____ tens is _____.

_____

4.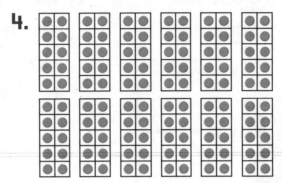

_____ tens is _____.

_____

5.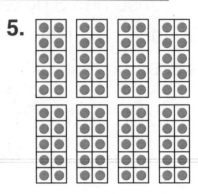

_____ tens is _____.

_____

Write the missing numbers.

6. **Number Sense** Jake wrote a pattern.

He forgot to write some numbers.

What numbers did Jake forget to write?

10, 20, 30, 40, _____, 60, _____, _____, 90, 100, _____, 120

7. **Model** José has 3 boxes. 10 books are in each box. How many books does José have in all?

_____ tens

_____

_____

8. **Model** Juan has 4 boxes. There are 10 books in each box. How many books does Juan have in all?

_____ tens

_____

9. **Higher Order Thinking** Dan counts by 5s to 50. Ed counts by 10s to 50. Write the numbers Dan says.

5, _____, _____, _____, _____, _____, _____, _____, _____, 50

Write the numbers Ed says.

10, _____, _____, _____, 50

What numbers do both boys say?

_____, _____, _____, _____, _____

10. ☑ **Assessment Practice** Mary has some books. She puts them in piles of 10 without any left over. Which number does **NOT** show how many books Mary could have?

(A) 50

(B) 60

(C) 65

(D) 70

Activity

Lesson 7-2
Count by 1s
to 120

I can ...
count by 1s to 120.

I can also be precise
in my work.

Name _____

Solve & Share

Help Alex decide what to say
after Jada stops counting.
Circle the correct one.
Explain why that one works.

98, 99, 100

_____ , _____ , _____

110, 111, 112?

110, 120, 130?

101, 102, 103?

This block shows 100. You say one hundred for this number.

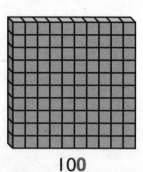

100

The next number you say is one hundred one because you have 1 hundred and 1 one.

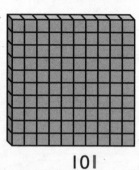

101

When you count forward, you keep counting by 1s.

101, 102, 103, 104, 105

105 means 1 hundred and 5 ones. You say one hundred five.

When you count higher, you start with the words one hundred.

116, 117, 118, 119, 120

116 is one hundred sixteen.

Convince Me! How would you say and show 110 when you count? What number comes next?

☆ Guided Practice ☆ Count forward by 1s. Write the numbers.

1. 116, _117_, 118, _119_, _120_

2. _____, 110, _____, _____, 113

3. 104, _____, _____, 107, _____

Topic 7 | Lesson 2

Name _____

Independent Practice ✩ Count forward by 1s. Write the numbers.

4. 110, _____, _____, _____, 114

5. 52, _____, _____, 55, _____

6. _____, 94, _____, 96, _____

7. _____, 102, 103, _____, _____

8. _____, _____, 115, _____, 117

9. 67, _____, _____, _____, 71

Number Sense Use the clues to find each mystery number.

10. Clue 1: The number comes after 116.
Clue 2: The number comes before 120.
The mystery number might be:

_____, _____, _____

Clue 3: The number has 8 ones.
Circle the mystery number.

11. Clue 1: The number comes before 108.
Clue 2: The number comes after 102.
The mystery number might be:

_____, _____, _____, _____, _____

Clue 3: The number has 5 ones.
Circle the mystery number.

12. (A-Z) **Vocabulary** Marta is counting to 120. She says the number that is one **more** than 113. What number does she say?

13. In this chart, Tom writes the numbers 102 to 108 in order. Some numbers rub off. Help Tom fill in the missing numbers.

102		104	105			108

14. **Reasoning** Shelly counts 109 bottle caps. Then she counts 4 more. How many bottle caps has Shelley counted?

_____ bottle caps

Think about the numbers you count on.

15. **Higher Order Thinking** Pick a number greater than 99 and less than 112. Write the number in the box.

Then write the three numbers that come before it and the number that comes after it.

_____ , _____ , _____ , [　　] , _____

16. ☑ **Assessment Practice** Which shows the correct order for counting forward by 1s? Choose two that apply.

☐ 103, 104, 105, 102

☐ 117, 118, 119, 120

☐ 101, 102, 103, 104

☐ 114, 112, 110, 108

Name _____

Solve & Share

Pick a number. Write the number in the box.

How can you find the number that is 1 more?

Write that number. Then write the next 3 numbers.

1	2	3	4	5	6	7	8	9	10
11	12	13	14	15	16	17	18	19	20
21	22	23	24	25	26	27	28	29	30
31	32	33	34	35	36	37	38	39	40
41	42	43	44	45	46	47	48	49	50
51	52	53	54	55	56	57	58	59	60
61	62	63	64	65	66	67	68	69	70
71	72	73	74	75	76	77	78	79	80
81	82	83	84	85	86	87	88	89	90
91	92	93	94	95	96	97	98	99	100

☐ _____, _____, _____, _____

You can find patterns when you count forward on a **hundred chart**.

1	2	3	4	5	6	7	8	9	10
11	12	13	14	15	16	17	18	19	20
21	22	23	24	25	26	27	28	29	30
31	32	33	34	35	36	37	38	39	40
41	42	43	44	45	46	47	48	49	50
51	52	53	54	55	56	57	58	59	60
61	62	63	64	65	66	67	68	69	70
71	72	73	74	75	76	77	78	79	80
81	82	83	84	85	86	87	88	89	90
91	92	93	94	95	96	97	98	99	100

The tens digit in each number in this row is 1.

1	2	3	4
11	12	13	14
21	22	23	24
31	32	33	34

The ones digit in each number in this column is 4.

1	2	3	4
11	12	13	14
21	22	23	24
31	32	33	34

A number chart can extend past 100 to greater numbers.

81	82	83	84	85	86	87	88	89	90
91	92	93	94	95	96	97	98	99	100
101	102	103	104	105	106	107	108	109	110
111	112	113	114	115	116	117	118	119	120

The numbers past 100 follow the same pattern.

Convince Me! How do the numbers in a number chart change?

☆ **Guided Practice** ☆ Count by 1s. Write the numbers. Use a number chart to help you.

1. 14, _15_, _16_, _17_, _18_

2. 21, _____, _____, _____, _____

3. 103, _____, _____, _____, _____

4. _____, _____, 49, _____, _____

Independent Practice ☆ Count by 1s. Write the numbers. Use a number chart to help you.

5. _____, 65, _____, _____, _____

6. _____, 52, _____, _____, _____

7. _____, _____, 83, _____, _____

8. 110, _____, _____, _____, _____

9. _____, _____, _____, _____, 79

10. _____, _____, _____, _____, 98

11. _____, _____, _____, _____, 91

12. _____, _____, _____, 102, _____

Higher Order Thinking Look at each partial number chart. Write the missing numbers.

13.

34		36	
	45		47

14.

	98		
107			110

1	2	3	4	5	6	7	8	9	10
11	12	13	14	15	16	17	18	19	20
21	22	23	24	25	26	27	28	29	30
31	32	33	34	35	36	37	38	39	40
41	42	43	44	45	46	47	48	49	50
51	52	53	54	55	56	57	58	59	60
61	62	63	64	65	66	67	68	69	70
71	72	73	74	75	76	77	78	79	80
81	82	83	84	85	86	87	88	89	90
91	92	93	94	95	96	97	98	99	100
101	102	103	104	105	106	107	108	109	110
111	112	113	114	115	116	117	118	119	120

15. **Use Tools** Billy counts forward to 50. What are the next 5 numbers he counts? Write the numbers.

50, _____, _____, _____, _____, _____

16. **Use Tools** Sasha counts forward to 115. What are the next 5 numbers she counts? Write the numbers.

115, _____, _____, _____, _____, _____

17. **Higher Order Thinking** Pick a number from the number chart. Count forward. Write the numbers.

_____, _____, _____, _____, _____,

_____, _____, _____, _____, _____

18. ☑ **Assessment Practice** Draw an arrow to match the missing number to the number chart.

| 75 | | 100 | | 101 | | 114 |

| 112 | 113 | | 115 | 116 | 117 | 118 |

Name _____

Count by 10s, starting at 10. Color the numbers you count yellow. What pattern do you see? Count by 1s, starting at 102. Draw a red square around the numbers. Count by 10s, starting at 34. Draw a blue circle around the numbers. Describe the patterns for each.

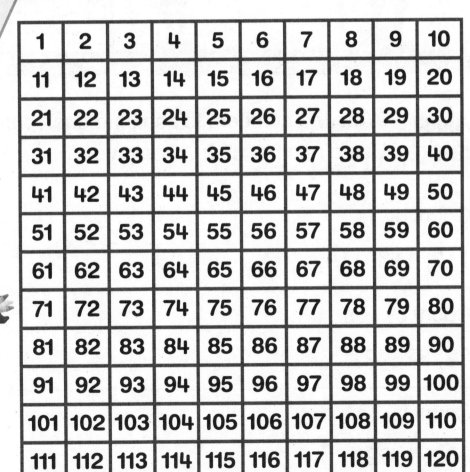

1	2	3	4	5	6	7	8	9	10
11	12	13	14	15	16	17	18	19	20
21	22	23	24	25	26	27	28	29	30
31	32	33	34	35	36	37	38	39	40
41	42	43	44	45	46	47	48	49	50
51	52	53	54	55	56	57	58	59	60
61	62	63	64	65	66	67	68	69	70
71	72	73	74	75	76	77	78	79	80
81	82	83	84	85	86	87	88	89	90
91	92	93	94	95	96	97	98	99	100
101	102	103	104	105	106	107	108	109	110
111	112	113	114	115	116	117	118	119	120

You can count on a number chart to find a pattern.

1	2	3	4	5	6	7	8	9	10
11	12	13	14	15	16	17	18	19	20
21	22	23	24	25	26	27	28	29	30
31	32	33	34	35	36	37	38	39	40
41	42	43	44	45	46	47	48	49	50
51	52	53	54	55	56	57	58	59	60
61	62	63	64	65	66	67	68	69	70
71	72	73	74	75	76	77	78	79	80
81	82	83	84	85	86	87	88	89	90
91	92	93	94	95	96	97	98	99	100
101	102	103	104	105	106	107	108	109	110
111	112	113	114	115	116	117	118	119	120

Count by 10s.

10, 20, 30, 40

1	2	3	4	5	6	7	8	9	10
11	12	13	14	15	16	17	18	19	20
21	22	23	24	25	26	27	28	29	30
31	32	33	34	35	36	37	38	39	40

Count by 1s from 58 to 61.

58, 59, 60, 61

41	42	43	44	45	46	47	48	49	50
51	52	53	54	55	56	57	58	59	60
61	62	63	64	65	66	67	68	69	70
71	72	73	74	75	76	77	78	79	80

Count by 10s, starting at 84.

84, 94, 104, 114

81	82	83	84	85	86	87	88	89	90
91	92	93	94	95	96	97	98	99	100
101	102	103	104	105	106	107	108	109	110
111	112	113	114	115	116	117	118	119	120

Convince Me! Compare counting by 1s and by 10s. How are the patterns alike? How are the patterns different?

☆ **Guided Practice** ☆ Write the numbers to continue each pattern. Use a number chart to help you.

1. Count by 1s.

   112, 113, 114, _115_, _116_, _117_, _118_, _119_, _120_

2. Count by 10s.

   22, 32, 42, _____, _____, _____, _____, _____, _____

3. Count by 1s.

   90, 91, 92, _____, _____, _____, _____, _____

Topic 7 | Lesson 4

Name _____

Independent Practice Write the numbers to continue each pattern.
Use a number chart to help you.

4. Count by 10s.

10, 20, 30, _____ , _____ , _____ , _____ , _____ , _____ , _____ , _____ ,

5. Count by 10s.

35, 45, 55, _____ , _____ , _____ , _____ , _____ , _____

6. Count by 1s.

102, 103, 104, _____ , _____ , _____ , _____ , _____ , _____ , _____ ,

Number Sense Write the missing numbers on the number chart below.
Then write the next three numbers in the pattern you started. Explain.

7.

	62	63	64	65	66	67	68	69	70
	72	73	74	75	76	77	78	79	80
	82	83	84	85	86	87	88	89	90

_____ , _____ , _____ ,

8. Look for Patterns Anita walks her neighbor's dog to earn money. She starts on Day 13 and walks the dog once a day through Day 19. How many times does Anita walk the dog?

_____ times

1	2	3	4	5	6	7	8	9	10
11	12	13	14	15	16	17	18	19	20

9. Look for Patterns Matt starts swimming lessons on Day 5. He goes every 10 days. How many lessons will Matt go to in 30 days?

_____ lessons

1	2	3	4	5	6	7	8	9	10
11	12	13	14	15	16	17	18	19	20
21	22	23	24	25	26	27	28	29	30

Explain the pattern.

10. Higher Order Thinking Anna counts to 30. She only counts 3 numbers. Did Anna count by 1s or 10s? Use pictures, numbers, or words to explain.

11. ☑ Assessment Practice Tim counts by 10s, starting at 54.

54, 74, 84, 94, 114

What numbers did Tim forget to count?

Name _____

Solve & Share

Use the open number line to show how to count from 78 to 84.

I can ...
count to 120 using an open number line.

I can also model with math.

↔
|
78

You can use an open number line to count on by 1s.

Count on by 1s from 97 to 103.

+1 +1 +1 +1 +1 +1
97 98 99 100 101 102 103

97

I count the jumps by 1s until I get to 103!

You can use an open number line to count on by 10s.

Count on by 10s from 56 to 116.

+10 +10 +10 +10 +10 +10
56 66 76 86 96 106 116

56

I count the jumps by 10s until I get to 116!

Convince Me! Use an open number line. What number comes after 109 when you count on by 1s?
What number comes after 109 when you count on by 10s?

☆ **Guided Practice** Show your counting on the open number line.

1. Start at 99. Count on by 1s to 105.

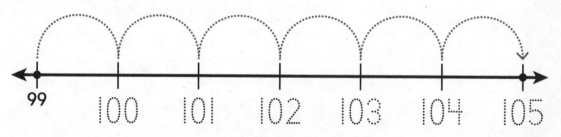

99 100 101 102 103 104 105

2. Start at 72. Count on by 10s to 112.

72

Tools   Assessment

Independent Practice ☆   Show your counting on the open number line.

3. Start at 89. Count on
by 10s to 119.

4. Start at 111. Count
on by 1s to 118.

5. Number Sense Teresa and Doug both draw a number line starting at 27.
Teresa counts on by 1s five times. Doug counts on by 10s five times.

Will they stop counting at the same number? Explain.

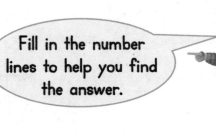

27   27

Teresa   Doug

Fill in the number
lines to help you find
the answer.

_____

_____

_____

6. **Model** Dennis counts 41 marbles. Then he counts 8 more marbles.
   How many marbles did he count in all?

   _____ marbles

   41

7. **Higher Order Thinking** On Monday, Kate puts 12 pennies in her piggy bank.
   On Tuesday, she puts some more pennies in her bank.
   She puts 19 pennies in all in her bank.
   How many pennies did she put in her bank on Tuesday?

   _____ pennies

   12

8. ☑ **Assessment Practice** Tim showed his counting on this number line.
   Complete the sentence to show how he counted.

   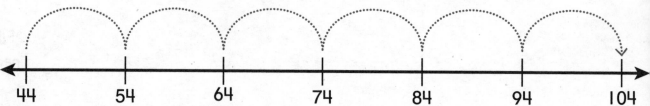

   44   54   64   74   84   94   104

   Tim counted by _____ from _____ to _____.

Activity

Solve & Share

Look at the oranges below. Count to find out how many in all and then write the number. Explain how you counted the oranges.

I can ...
write a numeral to show how many objects are in the group.

I can also use repeated reasoning.

There are _____ oranges.

How many stickers are shown?

What is the best way to count this many stickers?

You can count by 1s.

1	2	3	4	5	6	7	8	9	10
11	12	13	14	15	16	17	18	19	20
21	22	23	24	25	26	27	28	29	30
31	32	33	34	35	36	37	38	39	40
41									

There are 41 stickers!

You can also count by 10s.

10
20
30
40
41

I can count 10, 20, 30, 40. Then I add the 1 left to get 41 stickers.

Convince Me! Start at 19 and count on 6 more. Then write the numeral that you ended on.

☆ **Guided Practice** ☆ Count the objects any way you choose. Then write how many in all.

1.

4̲6̲ balls

2.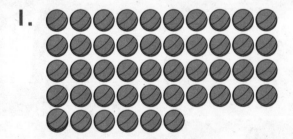

_____ rabbits

Name _____

Independent Practice   Count the objects. Then write how many in all.

3.

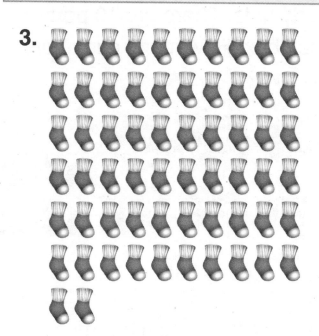

_____ socks

4.

_____ bananas

Use place-value blocks to count the tens and ones. Then write how many in all.

5.

_____ tens _____ ones

_____ in all

6.

_____ tens _____ ones

_____ in all

7.

_____ tens _____ ones

_____ in all

8. Reasoning Daniel finds 3 boxes of teddy bears and 4 more teddy bears. Each box holds 10 teddy bears. How many teddy bears did Daniel find?

Daniel found _____ teddy bears.

9. Reasoning Kim has 8 boxes and 6 more party hats. There are 10 party hats in each box. How many party hats does Kim have?

Kim has _____ party hats.

10. Higher Order Thinking Write the number of objects you see. Tell how you counted them.

_____

_____

11. ☑ Assessment Practice How many strawberries are shown below?

Ⓐ 18

Ⓑ 24

Ⓒ 26

Ⓓ 62

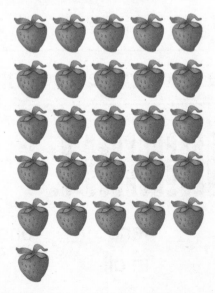

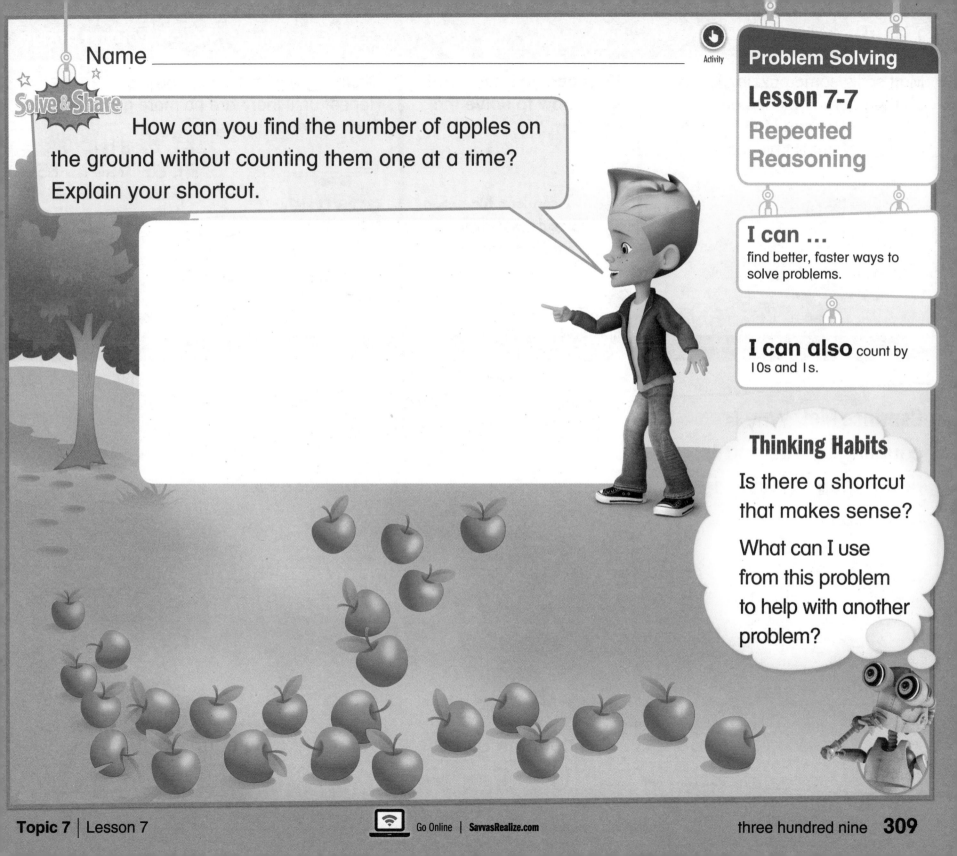

Name _____

Solve & Share

How can you find the number of apples on the ground without counting them one at a time? Explain your shortcut.

I can ...
find better, faster ways to solve problems.

I can also count by 10s and 1s.

Thinking Habits

Is there a shortcut that makes sense?

What can I use from this problem to help with another problem?

Matt spills some puzzle pieces on the floor. 61 pieces are still in the box. How can Matt find the number of puzzle pieces in all?

How can you use what you know to solve the problem?

I can look for shortcuts and things that repeat.

Circle a group of 10 and count on. Repeat until there are no more groups of 10. Then count on by 1s.

61, 71, 81, 82, 83, 84, 85. There are 85 puzzle pieces in all.

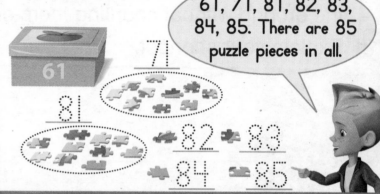

Convince Me! Why is counting by 10s and 1s better than counting 1 at a time?

⭐ **Guided Practice** ⭐ How many in all? Use a shortcut to count on. Tell what shortcut you used.

1.
30 shoes

58 shoes

I counted on by
10s and 1s .

2.
60 muffins

_____ muffins

I counted on by
_____ .

Topic 7 | Lesson 7

Tools   Assessment

Independent Practice

How many in all? Use a shortcut to count on.
Tell what shortcut you used.

3.

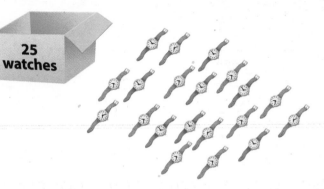

25 watches

_____ watches

I counted on by _____.

4.

32 train cars

_____ train cars

I counted on by _____.

5.

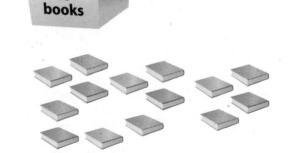

45 books

_____ books

I counted on by _____.

6.

30 desks

_____ desks

I counted on by _____.

Problem Solving

Students and Snowmen

62 students stay inside at recess. The rest each build a snowman outside. How can you count to find the number of students in all?

62 students

7. Make Sense What do you know about the students? What do you need to find?

_____

_____

_____

8. Reasoning What does the number of snowmen tell me?

_____

_____

_____

9. Generalize How many students in all? What shortcut did you use to find the answer?

_____

_____

_____

_____

_____

_____

Show the Word

Color these sums and differences. Leave the rest white.

| 8 | 5 | 6 |

I can ... add and subtract within 10.

I can also be precise in my work.

4 + 2	5 − 3	0 + 6	6 + 2	8 + 0	7 + 1	8 − 3	7 − 2	1 + 4
9 − 3	10 − 3	8 − 2	10 − 2	2 − 2	2 + 6	2 + 3	2 + 2	6 − 1
10 − 4	6 + 0	3 + 3	1 + 7	10 − 7	3 + 5	0 + 5	5 − 0	3 + 2
5 + 1	1 + 1	2 + 4	5 + 3	9 − 5	9 − 1	4 + 1	1 + 2	9 − 7
7 − 1	1 − 1	6 − 0	8 − 0	4 + 4	0 + 8	10 − 5	9 − 0	5 − 2

The word is

_____ _____ _____

A-Z
Glossary

Word List
- column
- hundred chart
- number chart
- ones digit
- row
- tens digit

Understand Vocabulary

1. Circle the number that shows the ones digit.

106

2. Circle the number that shows the tens digit.

106

3. Circle a column in the part of the hundred chart.

87	88	89	90
97	98	99	100

4. Circle a row in the part of the number chart.

107	108	109	110
117	118	119	120

5. Circle the number on the chart that is 1 more than 101.

97	98	99	100
101	102	103	104

Use Vocabulary in Writing

6. Fill in the number chart to count on from 95 to 106. Explain the difference between a number chart and a hundred chart. Label the chart using words from the Word List.

91	92	93	94	95					
					106	107	108	109	110

_____

_____

_____

Name _____

Set A _____

You can count by 10s when you have a lot of objects to count.

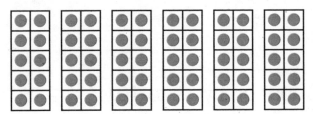

There are ___6___ tens.

6 tens = ___60___

The word name for 60 is ___sixty___.

Count by 10s. Write the number 3 different ways.

1.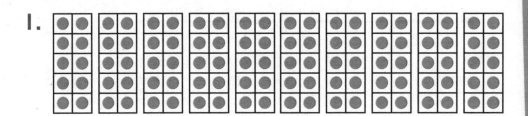

_____ tens

number: _____

word name: _____

Set B _____

You can use a number chart to count on by 1s or 10s.

81	82	83	84	85	86	87	88	89	90
91	92	93	94	95	96	97	98	99	100
101	102	103	104	105	106	107	108	109	110
111	112	113	114	115	116	117	118	119	120

Count on by 1s.

99, 100, ___101___, ___102___, ___103___

Use a number chart to count on.

2. Count by 10s.

80, _____, _____, _____, _____

3. Count by 1s.

114, _____, _____, _____, _____

You can use an open number line to count on by 1s or 10s.

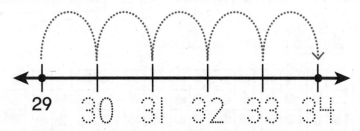

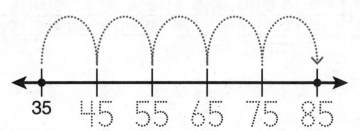

Count on using the open number line.

4. Start at 62. Count on by 10s to 102.

5. Start at 97. Count on by 1s to 101.

Thinking Habits

Repeated Reasoning

Does something repeat in the problem? How does that help?

Is there a shortcut that makes sense?

Count on by a number to find how many in all.

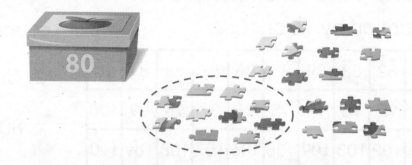

6. Eighty puzzle pieces are in the box. How many puzzle pieces are there in all? Explain how you counted.

_____ pieces

Name _____

1. Count by 10s. What number is shown?
Write the number 3 different ways.

_____ tens

number: _____

word name: _____

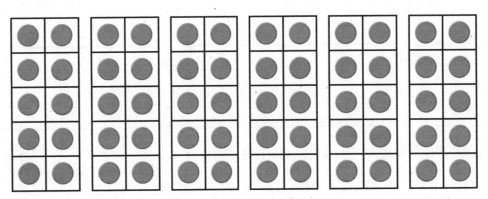

Use the partial number chart below to solve each problem.

91	92	93	94	95	96	97	98	99	100
101	102	103	104	105	106	107	108	109	110
111	112	113	114	115	116	117	118	119	120

2. Cathy counts pennies by 1s.
She counts to 98. Which number will
Cathy say next?

89   90   99   108
Ⓐ   Ⓑ   Ⓒ   Ⓓ

3. Sam counts by 10s.

80, 90, 100, 120

Which number did he forget to count?

89   105   110   115
Ⓐ   Ⓑ   Ⓒ   Ⓓ

4. Start at 58. Count on by 10s to 98.

5. Start at 114. Count on by 1s to 118.

6. Alex sees some baby chicks at the farm. 50 chicks are in the hen house. How many baby chicks in all? Use the picture to solve.

Ⓐ 68

Ⓑ 72

Ⓒ 78

Ⓓ 80

7. The farm worker says there are 82 chicks this morning. Some of the chicks are hiding. How many chicks are hiding? Use your answer from Item 6 to solve. Then explain how you know.

Name _____

Maya's Marbles

Maya collects marbles and keeps them in jars.

1. How many blue marbles does Maya have?
Circle groups of 10. Then count by 10s.
Write the numbers and the number word.

⚫ ⚫ ⚫ ⚫ ⚫ ⚫ ⚫ ⚫ ⚫ ⚫

⚫ ⚫ ⚫ ⚫ ⚫ ⚫ ⚫ ⚫ ⚫ ⚫

⚫ ⚫ ⚫ ⚫ ⚫ ⚫ ⚫ ⚫ ⚫ ⚫

⚫ ⚫ ⚫ ⚫ ⚫ ⚫ ⚫ ⚫ ⚫ ⚫

⚫ ⚫ ⚫ ⚫ ⚫ ⚫ ⚫ ⚫ ⚫ ⚫

_____ groups of 10 marbles

_____ marbles

_____ marbles

2. Maya has some striped marbles. Use these clues to find out how many she has.

Clue 1: The number comes after 110.

Clue 2: The number comes before 120.

Clue 3: The number does **NOT** have 4 ones.

Clue 4: The number in the ones place is the same as the number in the tens place.

Maya has _____ striped marbles.

3. Maya has 105 small marbles in a jar. She puts 13 more small marbles in the jar. How many small marbles are in the jar now?

Solve using the number line or part of the number chart. Then explain how you solved.

81	82	83	84	85	86	87	88	89	90
91	92	93	94	95	96	97	98	99	100
101	102	103	104	105	106	107	108	109	110
111	112	113	114	115	116	117	118	119	120

_____

_____

_____

There are _____ small marbles in the jar.

4. Maya has 48 large marbles in a jar. There are more large marbles on the floor. How can you count to find how many large marbles Maya has in all?

48 marbles

What do you know about the large marbles?

_____

_____

What shortcut did you use to count the marbles? Tell how you counted.

_____

_____

_____

Maya has _____ large marbles in all.

Glossary

I less

4 is I less than 5.

I more

5 is I more than 4.

10 less

20 is 10 less than 30.

10 more

10 more than a number has I more ten or 10 more ones.

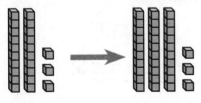

add

When you add, you find out how many there are in all.

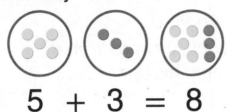

$$5 + 3 = 8$$

addend

the numbers you add together to find the whole

$$2 + 3 = 5$$

addition equation

$$3 + 4 = 7$$

addition fact

$$9 + 8 = 17$$

attribute

something about a type of shape that helps define that shape

break apart

to separate a number into two parts

Tens	Ones

43 is 4 tens and 3 ones.

C

cent (¢)

a unit value of money for coins

column

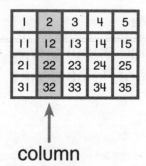

1	2	3	4	5
11	12	13	14	15
21	22	23	24	25
31	32	33	34	35

↑
column

compare

to find out how things are alike or different

cone

count back

to count backward from a number by 1s or 10s.

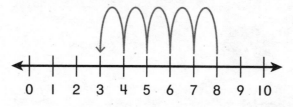

8, 7, 6, 5, 4, 3

count on

to count forward from a number by 1s or 10s.

15, _16_, _17_, _18_

20, _30_, _40_, _50_

cube

cylinder

D

data

information you collect

Favorite Pets
cat
dog
cat
cat
dog

difference

the amount that is left after you subtract

$$4 - 1 = 3$$

The difference is 3.

digits

Numbers have 1 or more digits.

43 has 2 digits.
The tens digit is 4.
The ones digit is 3.

43

dime

a coin that has a value of 10 cents (10¢)

front   back

dollar

usually a paper money that has a value of 100 cents

front   back

doubles fact

an addition fact with the same addends

$$4 + 4 = 8$$

4 and 4 is a double.

doubles-plus fact

an addition fact with addends that are 1 apart or 2 apart

$$\underbrace{3 + 4}_{addends} = 7$$

$$\underbrace{3 + 5}_{addends} = 8$$

edges

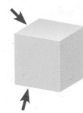

equal shares

4 equal parts

equal sign (=)

$$2 + 3 = 5$$

equal sign

equals

have the same value; 5 + 2 equals 7.

equation

a math sentence that has an equal sign

$6 + 4 = 10$ $6 - 2 = 4$

$10 = 6 + 4$ $4 = 6 - 2$

F

faces

fact family

a group of related addition and subtraction facts

$3 + 5 = 8$
$5 + 3 = 8$
$8 - 3 = 5$
$8 - 5 = 3$

fewer

less in number

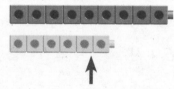

The yellow row has fewer cubes.

---

flat surface

---

fourths

The square is divided into fourths.

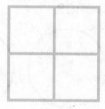

G

greater than (>)

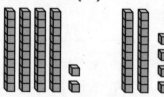

42 is greater than 24.

Compare: 42 > 24

---

greatest

the number or group with the largest value

| 7 | 11 | 23 |

23 is the greatest number.

H

half hour

A half hour is 30 minutes.

1:30

---

halves

The circle is divided into halves.

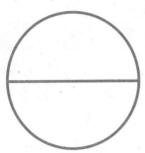

hexagon

hour

An hour is 60 minutes.

2:00

hour hand

The short hand on a clock is the hour hand.
The hour hand tells the hour.

It is 3:00.

hour hand

hundred chart

A hundred chart shows all of the numbers from 1 to 100.

1	2	3	4	5	6	7	8	9	10
11	12	13	14	15	16	17	18	19	20
21	22	23	24	25	26	27	28	29	30
31	32	33	34	35	36	37	38	39	40
41	42	43	44	45	46	47	48	49	50
51	52	53	54	55	56	57	58	59	60
61	62	63	64	65	66	67	68	69	70
71	72	73	74	75	76	77	78	79	80
81	82	83	84	85	86	87	88	89	90
91	92	93	94	95	96	97	98	99	100

in all

There are 4 birds in all.

inside

The dogs are inside the dog house.

join

to put together

3 and 3 is 6 in all.

L

least

the number or group with the smallest value

7	11	23

7 is the least number.

length

the distance from one end of an object to the other end

less

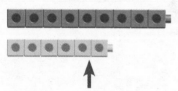

The number of cubes in the yellow row is less.

less than (<)

24 is less than 42.

Compare: 24 < 42

longer

An object that is 7 cubes long is longer than an object that is 2 cubes long.

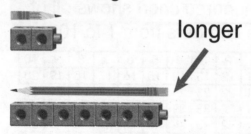

longer

longest

The object that takes the most units to measure is the longest.

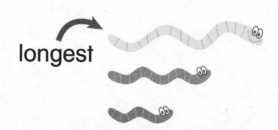

longest

M

make 10

$7 + 4 = ?$

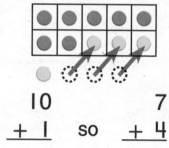

$$10 \quad\quad\quad 7$$
$$\underline{+\ 1} \quad so \quad \underline{+\ 4}$$
$$11 \quad\quad\quad 11$$

measure

You can measure length with same-size length units. The marker is 3 paper clips long.

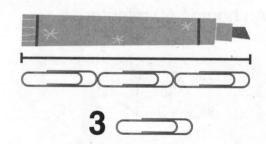

3

minus

$$5 - 3$$

5 minus 3

This means 3 is taken away from 5.

minus sign (–)

$$7 - 4 = 3$$
   ⬆

minute

60 minutes is 1 hour.

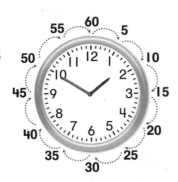

minute hand

The long hand on a clock is the minute hand.
The minute hand tells the minutes.

minute hand

It is 3:00.

missing part

the part that is not known

5

?

2 is the missing part.

more

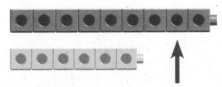

The red row has more cubes.

N

near double

an addition fact that has an addend that is 1 or 2 more than the other addend

$$4 + 5 = 9$$

$4 + 4 = 8$. 8 and 1 more is 9.

nickel

a coin that has a value of 5 cents (5¢)

front   back

number chart

A number chart can show numbers past 100.

81	82	83	84	85	86	87	88	89	90
91	92	93	94	95	96	97	98	99	100
101	102	103	104	105	106	107	108	109	110
111	112	113	114	115	116	117	118	119	120

number line

A number line is a line that shows numbers in order from left to right.

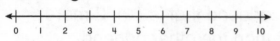

o'clock

8:00
8 o'clock

ones

single units

 2 ones

ones digit

The ones digit in 43 is 3.

ones digit

open number line

An open number line is a number line without marks in place.

order

60   61   62   63

least   greatest

Numbers can be put in counting order from least to greatest or from greatest to least.

outside

5 dogs are playing outside of the dog house.

part

a piece of a whole

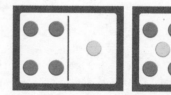

2 and 3 are parts of 5.

pattern

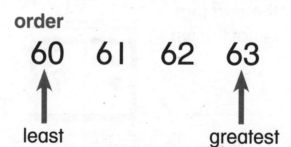

You can arrange 5 objects in any pattern, and there will still be 5 objects.

G8

penny

a coin that has a value of 1 cent (1¢)

front   back

picture graph

a graph that uses pictures to show data

Favorite Pets			
🐱 Cat	🐱	🐱	🐱
🐶 Dog	🐶	🐶	

plus

$$5 + 4$$

5 plus 4

This means 4 is added to 5.

plus sign (+)

$$6 + 2 = 8$$

quarter

a coin that has a value of 25 cents (25¢)

front   back

quarters

The square is divided into quarters, another word for fourths.

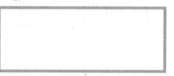

rectangle

rectangular prism

related facts

addition facts and subtraction facts that have the same numbers

$$2 + 3 = 5$$
$$5 - 2 = 3$$

These facts are related.

row

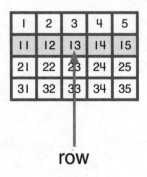

row

shorter

An object that is 2 cubes long is shorter than one that is 7 cubes long.

 shorter

shortest

The shortest object is the one that takes the fewest units to measure.

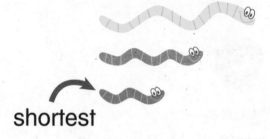

shortest

side

These shapes have straight sides.

sort

to group objects according to how they are similar

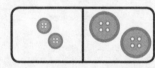

The buttons are sorted by size.

sphere

square

standard form

a number shown in digits

28

straws

A same-size unit used to measure length.

subtract

When you subtract, you find out how many are left.

$5 - 3 = 2$

subtraction equation

$12 - 4 = 8$

sum

$2 + 3 = 5$

↑
sum

survey

to gather information

Do you like cats or dogs better?

Cats |||
Dogs ||

T

take away

Start With	Take Away	Have Left
6	3	3

$6 - 3 = 3$

To take away is to remove or subtract.

tally chart

a chart that uses marks to show data

Walk	School Bus

tally marks

marks used to show the number of objects in groups of 5s

ten

one group of 10

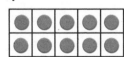

tens digit

The tens digit shows how many groups of 10 are in a number.

 35 has 3 tens.

35

Three-dimensional (3-D) shapes

These are all 3-D shapes.

trapezoid

triangle

Two-dimensional (2-D) shapes

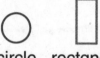

circle   rectangle   square   triangle

vertex (vertices)

a corner point where the edges or sides of 3-D or 2-D shapes meet

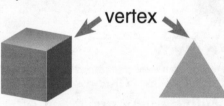

vertex

whole

You add parts to find the whole.

5

The whole is 5.

enVision® Mathematics

Photographs

Every effort has been made to secure permission and provide appropriate credit for photographic material. The publisher deeply regrets any omission and pledges to correct errors called to its attention in subsequent editions.

Unless otherwise acknowledged, all photographs are the property of Savvas Learning Company LLC.

Photo locators denoted as follows: Top (T), Center (C), Bottom (B), Left (L), Right (R), Background (Bkgd)

1 MattiaATH/Shutterstock; **3** (T) Shawn Hempel/Shutterstock, (C) Apiguide/Shutterstock, (B) Jennifer Photography Imaging/iStock/Getty Images; **4** (Bkgrd) ESB Professional/Shutterstock, Nancy Hixson/Shutterstock; **53** Karen Faljyan/Shutterstock; **55** (T) Images-USA/Alamy Stock Photo, (B) Scott Prokop/Shutterstock; **56** (T) NASA, (B) Blickwinkel/Alamy Stock Photo; **105** (L) Fotografie4you/Shutterstock, (R) Chris Sargent/Shutterstock; **107** (T) Blickwinkel/Alamy Stock Photo, (C) Alison Eckett/Alamy Stock Photo, (B) Racheal Grazias/Shutterstock; **108** (Bkgrd) Best Photo Studio/Shutterstock, Bay015/Shutterstock; **157** (L) FloridaStock/Shutterstock, (R) 611248/Shutterstock; **159** (T) Foodcollection/Getty Images, (B) DeymosHR/Shutterstock; **160** (T) Frank Romeo/Shutterstock, (B) Steve Heap/Shutterstock; **209** Willyam Bradberry/Shutterstock; **211** (T) Sanit Fuangnakhon/Shutterstock, (C) 123RF, (B) Art Vandalay/Digital Vision/Getty Images; **212** (Bkgrd) Wckiw/123RF, Valdis Torms/Shutterstock; **249** (L) Nick barounis/Fotolia, (C) Umberto Shtanzman/Shutterstock, (R) Gudellaphoto/Fotolia; **251** (T) PK-Photos/E+/Getty Images, (B) Kira Garmashova/Shutterstock; **252** (T) Rawpixel.com/Shutterstock, (B) Gary Corbett/Alamy Stock Photo; **281** John Foxx Collection/Imagestate/DK Images; **283** (T) PhotoAlto/Anne-Sophie Bost/Getty Images, (C) Lakov Filimonov/Shutterstock, (B) Melnikof/Shutterstock; **284** Rawpixel.com/Shutterstock, (B) Suwat Wongkham/Shutterstock; **321** (L) Chaoss/Fotolia, (R) Lipsett Photography Group/Shutterstock; **323** (T) Brent Hofacker/Shutterstock, (B) Prasit Rodphan/Shutterstock; **324** (T) Brent Hofacker/Shutterstock, (B) Kevin Schafer/Alamy Stock Photo; **361** Anton Petrus/Shutterstock; **363** (T) Anton Foltin/Shutterstock, (C) HD Cineman/iStock/Getty Images, (B) Markara/Shutterstock; **364** (Bkgrd) Nadya Eugene/Shutterstock, Mauro Rodrigues/Shutterstock; **397** (L) Baldas1950/Shutterstock, (R) Shooarts/Shutterstock; **399** (T) Brian J. Skerry/National Geographic/Getty Images, (B) Westend61/Getty Images; **400** (T) Lori Skelton/Shutterstock, (B) Andrea Izzotti/Shutterstock; **449** Yarek Gora/Shutterstock; **451** (T) Josh Cornish/Shutterstock, (C) Gregory Adams/Moment Open/Getty Images, (B) Shaun A Daley/Alamy Stock Photo; **452** (Bkgrd) I-m-a-g-e/Shutterstock, Yellow Cat/Shutterstock; **489** Studio 37/Shutterstock; **491** (T) Vojta Herout/Shutterstock, (B) Kohei Hara/Digital Vision/Getty Images; **492** (T) Light Field Studios/Shutterstock, (B) Studio 1One/Shutterstock; **517** Vereshchagin Dmitry/Shuhtterstock; **519** (T) George Rudy/Shutterstock, (C) People Image Studio/Shutterstock, (B) Sally and Richard Greenhill/Alamy Stock Photo; **520** (Bkgrd) 123RF, Maxop-Plus/Shutterstock; **553** Sergey Dzyuba/Shutterstock; **555** (T) Joyfull/Shutterstock, (B) R.Nagy/Shutterstock; **556** (T) Nattanan726/Shutterstock, (B) Roman Korotkov/Shutterstock; **605** (TL) Sumire8/Fotolia, (TR) Janifest/Fotolia, (BL) Isuaneye/Fotolia, (BR) Ftfoxfoto/Fotolia; **607** (T) Africa Studio/Shutterstock (C) Wollertz/Shutterstock, (B) Digitalpress/123RF; **612** (Bkgrd) Dmitry Melnikov/123RF, David Homen/Shutterstock, Melnikof/Shutterstock.